FREDDIE'S
LAST RIDE

'What Really Happened to Freddie Gray?'

by Mary Anne Whelan Ph.D. MD

DORRANCE
PUBLISHING CO
EST. 1920
PITTSBURGH, PENNSYLVANIA 15238

Dorrance Publishing Co
585 Alpha Drive
Suite 103
Pittsburgh, PA 15238
Visit our website at www.dorrancebookstore.com

ISBN: 978-1-6480-4259-1
eISBN: 978-1-6480-4910-1

ABOUT THIS BOOK

People have asked me – a lot – about why, given all the injustices of this world, I picked Freddie Gray to become particularly exercised about. It's because this one landed in my territory. And it was perfectly obvious to me, and the numerous neurologists and spine surgeons and other friends who had to listen to me carry on about it, that the arresting officers broke his neck; that the charges were largely misplaced, that there was a desert of investigative reporting, and that nobody who was placed to do so was speaking out or publicly reviewing it from a medical point of view. The sense of a void to fill became oppressive until I couldn't stand it any longer, something had to give, and I finally sat down and started to write about it in the effort to make whatever difference I could.

Concerning sources: I reviewed in detail literally thousands of pages of transcripts of the trials of the charged police officers, and investigative police files obtained under the Freedom of Information act. Student Maria Trovato provided some early research assistance. A good deal of information I have not specifically referenced because it is readily available from public sources: for example, Freddie Gray's arrest record, or demographic data, or nationwide data on police shootings. The Baltimore Sun reporting staff retrieved and published archived material on prior police cases of abuse in Baltimore, and also provided pertinent contemporaneous feature articles. They have been cited in the text, when quoted or heavily drawn on. Refences to specific findings and numerous topic-related papers in the medical literature can be ascertained and verified through the National Library of Medicine, *Entrez Pubmed*. Source books include Antero Pietila's *Not in My Neighborhood; Brown in Baltimore* by Howell S. Baum; *Human Lead Exposure* by Herbert Needleman. Statistical statements have generally been drawn from the websites of official Agencies and Departments of the State of Maryland or the City of Baltimore. The 2016 investigative report of the U.S. Department of Justice was an important source.

A number of persons declined requests for an interview. These included Forensic Pathologists Carol Allan, MD and her Chief, David Fowler, MD; Prosecuting Attorneys Janet Bledsoe and Michael Schatzow; Expert Witness Morris Soriano MD, and the office of Marilyn Mosby.

Many persons helped with encouragement - by providing guidance from their own experience, or inspiration by their own efforts and achievements, or of course both. Sometimes it was just a single encounter and comment, but at the right time and place. Writers and authors themselves (Paula DiPerna, Ginnah Howard, Betsy Peterson, Tazwell Thompson, Dolores Wharton), they knew what I was in for, but chose not to emphasize that side of things. Other persons did what they could to help in a practical sense (Faith Gay, Anne Marbury Wyatt-Brown, and the professional persons who at my request wrote the letters that met with the boiler-plate responses – especially I will mention neurologist Alexander Reeves, known as Alex the Great to his numerous medical students). Most of all I want to thank the dear friends who did not hastily remove themselves after a while or find other places to lunch or visit when they saw me coming: Dot and Harry Danner, Pat Gourlay and son John, Martha and Ed Heck, Sally McGuire Muspratt, David Newman, Bob and Diane Nicholls, Bill Oliver, Jamie Walker, Hilda and Sam Wilcox, Michael Willis. Journalist Ericka Blount Danois, in Baltimore, provided co-work, guidance and contributions throughout. She will probably write a book of her own.

While the book is of course heavily critical of the Baltimore Police Department, it is also dedicated to the many honorable and competent police officers, there and elsewhere, whose daily work and compassion have not been effaced by the often harsh realities of their daily encounters. Thanks for all you do for us.

Contents

CHAPTER 1:

The Setting of the Arrest

April 12, 2015 began as a Baltimore day much like any other, although it was a Sunday. The moon was less than half full. The weather was neither unseasonably warm, nor unseasonably cool – High 67, Low 33. There was no precipitation. The wind gusted up to 21 mph in this port town, but on the whole there was just some breeze, averaging 3 mph. In this setting, the police saw a young black man, Freddie Gray, and without provocation other than his identity chased him when he ran and pinned him when he stopped for them, slammed him face down, knelt on him, dragged him up and stuffed him into a police van. This, also, was not unusual. But on this occasion, rather unusually even for the Baltimore Police, they had broken his neck before stuffing him in. Forty minutes later he was dragged out dead, thereby becoming one of the 100 persons killed nationwide by police in April, 2015, and the sixth person to die in Baltimore police custody since 2012: Trayvon Scott, Maurice Johnson, Anthony Anderson, Tyrone West, George King and Freddie Gray all died while in the hands of the police. He was the fourth person of record since 1980 to die of a broken neck: John Wheatfall. Jeffrey Alston. Dondi Johnson. Freddie Gray. The official pronouncement of Gray's death, after his "resuscitation", took another 8 days. The cause of his death was given at autopsy as a broken neck. And the alleged timing of that event, as framed by the police and accepted by the Medical Examiner and hence the State Attorney for Baltimore

1

who brought the charges, was the single most critical factor in the miscarriage of justice that ensued, setting Baltimore on fire.

When the police arrested him on this fatal day there was no warrant out for his arrest, nor, apart from his running, was his behavior provocative or suspicious, but the police knew him well. He was 25, but he began being arrested at age 18. Most of the charges were for possession of marihuana, a couple for possession of a non-marihuana drug substance, and several for possession with intent to manufacture. He was charged with trespassing twice, and once for gaming – playing cards while sitting on someone's steps. Charges were dropped 9 times. When they were actually brought he was found guilty once and not guilty once. He was placed on probation twice. He was sentenced to jail only once, for a month and 11 days, for unlawful possession. Violence was not a part of his pattern, though he was once charged with assault, once with destruction of property and "unauthorized removal of property" – presumably, someone else's property, - and, most seriously, with intention to manufacture and distribute. These charges were dropped.

Several more recent charges, including two within the past month, were recorded as Abated By Death.

———

In 2016, the United States Department of Justice released its report entitled *Investigation of the Baltimore City Police Force.* This investigation had been undertaken at the request of Baltimore City Mayor Rawlings-Blake in the wake of Freddie Gray's death and the widespread protests spilling over into the destructive and injurious rioting that ensued. The report is most frequently referred to as "scathing". Nearly 200 pages long and meticulously documented, the Executive Summary read:

For the foregoing reasons, the Department of Justice concludes that there is reasonable cause to believe that the BPD {Baltimore Police Force} engages in a pattern or practice of conduct that violates the Constitution or federal law. The pattern or practice includes: (1) making unconstitutional stops, searches, and arrests; (2) using enforcement strategies that produce severe and unqualified disparities in the rates of stops, searches and arrests of African Americans; (3) using excessive force; and (4) retaliating against people engaged in constitutionally-protected expression. We also identified concerns regarding BPD's transport of individuals and investigations of sexual assaults. BPD's failings result from deficient policies, training, oversight, and accountability, and policing strategies that do not engage effectively with the community the Department serves.

All of these practices (except for the issue of sexual assaults) were manifest in the Gray case which, indeed, had stimulated the genesis of the report in the first place. The report did not specifically investigate the Gray incident: it was intended that that would subsequently be undertaken by the Justice Department as a Civil Rights case. (Begun by Attorney General of the United States Loretta Lynch during the Obama administration, it was killed by A.G. Jeff Sessions under Trump). It documents, among other things, the excessive frequency with which Blacks, particularly black males, were stopped or arrested without significant provocation – indisputably more frequently than Whites were, for the same offenses, and often for acts that would have met at most for reprimand had the perpetrators been white. Repetitive charges for "discretionary charges" – loitering, trespassing, spitting on the sidewalk – were common. One middle-aged black man was stopped 30 times in 4 months, without ever being charged. Another 7 black men were stopped more than 30 times. Another 34, more than 20 times. Although often stopped and arrested, even most Blacks were not subsequently charged – that would have wasted the time of busy courts. Between January and April of 2015 Baltimore City, with a population of 621,849, averaged 2,630 arrests a month. The population was 63% black, but the arrestees were 92% black. Marihuana use is reported to be about the same in both black and white populations, but black people were, and are, nearly 6 times as likely to be arrested for it. So if Freddie Gray had been picked up – again, for he had a history of more than 20 arrests, twice in the month of March alone in 2015- it probably would have gone unremarked, except by friends and family who sometimes bailed him out.

As for the use of inappropriate force, this was well recognized. The Baltimore Police Force had paid out literally millions of dollars in settlement cases in the two years preceding Gray's arrest.

Baltimore had not waited for the Department of Justice report to try to remedy the relationship between, especially, the black community and the police. In 1999 a Civilian Review Board (CRB) was established as an Independent City Agency within the Office of Equity and Civil Rights. It was composed of a citizen from each of the Baltimore City police districts, but those persons were appointed by the Mayor. There were also non-voting representatives, one each from the Vanguard Justice Society, the ACLU, the Baltimore City Branch of the NAACP, and the Baltimore City Police Commissioner or that person's designee. They were empowered to receive, investigate and in some sense handle complaints from the public about any and all aspects of police behavior, but they had no authority whatsoever. Sometimes even they or their family members were harassed by the police. The Police Commissioner decided whether or not to refer complaints against officers to an internal review board composed of police officers. The trial board did not share their decision-making with the CRB. The CRB could make recommendations, but they were non-binding. The police routinely ignored their subpoenas and otherwise withheld information. In 2015 a Baltimore City Citizen Review Board Coalition was formed by the President of the Matthew A. Henson Community Association, Marvin "Doc" Cheatham, to try to strengthen the CRB. It was composed of a former State Senator and several members of the Clergy but prayer seemed to get nowhere, so they subsequently took to the law and pushed to have civilians sit on the internal police trial board and to require police to share files about specific officers' misconduct, for public release. The appointed City Solicitor (2017-2020) Andre Davis, then given authority to represent both the Police and the CRB - a clear conflict of interest - said the CRB couldn't do that, but they did it anyway, and they won. The City Solicitor was enjoined 'From either advising and/or representing ...the CRB', and the Mayor was not to assign staff from the Solicitor's office to the CRB. Emboldened, the new Director of the Baltimore City Office of Civil Rights, Jill Carter, issued a report which would require two civilians to sit on the police trial board and allowing civilians to question and investigate police officers. She called for enhanced transparency and a bigger budget. Ultimately, she wanted the CRB to BE the trial board, but everyone knew that would never happen. Freddie Gray happened first and the lack of a transparent and independent investigation of his death was blamed by City Attorney General Mosby for the police acquittals.

———

Indeed the police knew Freddie Gray well: then 25, he had begun being arrested at 18, and had been arrested on average about 3 times a year ever since. He had been arrested twice in the month before his last, unprovoked, arrest. Freddie wasn't an angel, but he wasn't a real badass either. An elderly woman in his neighborhood, and a witness to the arrest, remembered him as someone who looked out for her and who was generous (when he had any money) to others. People liked him. He had some court-ordered community service, and was remembered as a good worker at the Fulton Heights Community Organization where he served. Clyde Boatwright, a Sargent for the Baltimore City Police Force who met Freddie at Carver High school, remembered him thus in speaking with Baltimore Journalist Ericka Blount Danois:

"I remember meeting Freddie as a high-school kid and people saying, 'This guy is pretty funny. He has a good sense of humor and he knows how to imitate people…I never had a bad interaction with Freddie in four years. If he chose his profession to be stand-up comedy, he would have been a natural: his impressions were perfect. He played on the football team, but he was a tiny kid and he didn't get a lot of playing time. One time he walked up next to the coach and made this sound like vroom, vroom. Coach was like 'What are you doing?' and Freddie he was like 'I'm like a Cadillac, ready to go!'"

On the fatal day of his arrest, therefore, if the question is not so much why the police went after him when they saw him coming away from a store where he had gone to get coffee with two friends – it was almost force of habit, for them – it becomes : why did Freddie run away? The question is perplexing to an outsider. There was no warrant out for his arrest. He was not in violation of probation. He had neither a weapon nor any illegal substance visibly on his person, nor, by laboratory testing at autopsy, did he have any drugs in his blood that were inconsistent with hospital administration, despite the media reporting otherwise. (A urine sample sent off at the time of admission did show marijuana and opioids, but he had been given Narcan by a Medic before transport and Narcan will result in a positive opioid test). In one of the several false narratives floated by the police, they claimed – and later had to retract the claim – that he had shown an illegal knife (at arrest, he did have a knife in his pocket, but it had not been shown and in any case the knife was a legal type). The police were therefore charged with false arrest. State Attorney Mosby bringing the charges should have known that that one, like most of the other charges, wouldn't stick. In excusing, first, the arrest, ultimately the Police could invoke two Supreme Court rulings justifying arrest. The first, Terry vs. Ohio (1968), justified BRIEF detainment for REASONABLE suspicion of illegal activity. This is frequently practiced in Baltimore, whose police seem to be a suspicious lot, albeit with some reason. There (and elsewhere) the stops are colloquially known as Terry stops. The ruling is the father (or Mother) of all "stop and frisk" policies, such as those practiced in New York City during the Bloomberg administration. Terry v. Ohio was expanded by subsequent rulings and interpretations, notably Illinois v. Wardlow (2000) which further loosened the definition of "reasonable" to essentially any probable cause, such as fleeing the police in a high-crime area. In general the majority of such arrests Nationwide have been dismissed, or the charges are dropped.

Given the reputation of the BPD and their interaction with Blacks – particularly young black males – taking off was perhaps an understandable, if ill-considered, impulse. One of the two friends with him, initially unnamed, took off also, but wasn't caught. Gray himself stopped running after a short while and let himself be captured. That was confirmed both by an eye-witness and the police. The police even said that he put himself down on the ground. That was a better idea, but that didn't work out well either. Despite the police claim that he was arrested "without undue force or incident," the first we see of him in the video of the arrest is that he is lying belly down on concrete, screaming in agony as one officer (who outweighs him by 100 lbs) kneels on his neck and the other grabs both legs by the ankles, lifts them up and forces them up towards the back of his head, thereby breaking his neck. Thereafter it took him less than an hour to die.

CHAPTER 2:

Why Did Freddie Run?
Executive Function and the Brain

`

Given the history of the BPD with regard to the arrest and frequently abusive history treatment of Blacks, it was perhaps not surprising that Freddie ran, but there was more to it than that. When Freddie first made eye contact with police Lieutenant Rice and decided to run, it could be described in general terms as a poor executive decision. To be sure, he ran because a lot of Blacks, especially young black men, are inclined to run away from the police. Collectively and individually there is a lot of negative prior experience. Witness to the arrest Michael Robinson, a friend of Gray's, said that Gray ran when seeing Rice because he had "a history with that police{man} beating him". Indeed Rice was not a gentle character: he had a history of having had his gun removed from him for mental health reasons, and had been the object of a domestic restraining order. One might say he was a bully with weapons and the authority to use them. But running away was still a poor executive decision.

Executive functions are those brain capabilities that enable people to make decisions based on reasoning and experience, and the ability to carry them out. They involve the synthesis of memory, learning abilities, thinking and decision-making. The tasks are different, of course, at different ages, and they apply to a broad range of situations, ranging from every-day mundane decisions about what to get in the market for dinner that night, or when to borrow money, or more far-reaching ones, such as whether to pull up in a no-stopping zone in front of the door of an Emergency Room when your or your wife is about to give birth, or whether or not to sell your company to Amazon for a couple of zillion dollars. At home, in school, and in the outside world, people learn whether it's a good idea to disobey an authority figure, and risk detention, or a beating, or jail – or not. Whether or not to start smoking, or try out the drugs which someone tells you will make you feel great, or not. Executive functions develop with age and experience of all kinds. At a later age, people may quit smoking, or get clean from drugs. One executive decision can over-ride another as evaluative capabilities develop. In the normal course of events school children do better than babies, and adolescents do better than toddlers, and better than elementary school students, but they do less well than normally matured adults.

Neurologically and anatomically, executive decision-making has been localized to the area of the brain known as the pre-frontal cortex. The brain however is interconnected in all its parts. The temporal lobes, for example, are the area of the brain which among other things are responsible for memory, but if temporal lobe damage should be so extensive that a person could not remember anything at all – and hence could not imprint experience, for future reference – then executive function would also be grossly impaired. The temporal lobes have inputs to the prefrontal cortex. So do the other parts of the brain, such as the parietal lobes, entrusted generally with a sense of direction. Did you ever make the executive decision to turn right instead of left, and end up in the middle of nowhere? You made a wrong executive decision, perhaps because your parietal lobes failed you in map reading, or your temporal lobes didn't remember that you had been told that the bridge was out, or your prefrontal cortex didn't put it together. Executive decisions can be tested for, by psychologists or other trained persons. And executive functions even if once acquired can be impaired, by head trauma, or severe psychological trauma, or exposure to a variety of toxins. They may be impaired short-term, so that you might do unwise things "under the influence" but not otherwise, or they might be impaired in some situations but not others. Veterans and others suffering from post-traumatic stress disorder may react to stimuli which recall the settings of their trauma and trigger reactions which are otherwise atypical for that person – getting in a fight or other violent behaviors, for example. Or executive functions can be impaired long-term - by the failure of the appropriate brain connections to develop, or because appropriate experience is lacking or distorted, or because of inhibition by any number of factors, even going back to prenatal exposures or the birth history itself. Marked prematurity is a risk factor for developmental delay or permanent cognitive impairment. A body of medical literature exists concerning the developmental outcomes, extending into adulthood, of fetuses exposed in utero to a variety of substances – opioids, or some medications used to block drug cravings and habituation, or alcohol (as in the well-recognized fetal alcohol syndrome). Although drug and alcohol use in pregnancy (and in general) are increased in populations with other pertinent factors, such as parental deficits in cognitive function, poor education, and all the other consequences and associations of poverty, there appears to be an independent and negative impact of these factors on child development. Placement of such children in foster care may lift the ongoing impact of poverty and its associations, but it does not fully negate the effects of prenatal exposure. In a study comparing exposed children to unexposed control babies, it was found that the exposed children (studied to eight and a half years), even if placed in adoptive or foster homes before the age of one, continued to have ongoing problems with cognitive abilities when compared to a control group if the mothers used heroin during pregnancy. It has also been found that both cognitive and behavioral difficulties persist into adult life. While educational approaches are at least potentially remedial, curative results are far from certain.

At the other end of the age spectrum, in old age executive function can be impaired by the generally progressive loss of brain capacities. Bad driving, inability to keep the check-book, making unrealistic commitments, gifts, investments, a lost ability in evaluating the motivation of others, or the consequences of certain actions, as those who prey upon the elderly well know – all these are examples of lost executive functional capabilities.

When Freddie chose to run, it showed poor executive function. It was a bad decision. And indeed he seemed, in a couple of minutes, to recognize that – he stopped and stood quietly for his arrest, according to one eyewitness and the police report. Of course, he had also been threatened with being tazed if he didn't, per the arresting officer's testimony. But running in the first place was a bad idea. What was wrong with his executive function? Why did Freddie Run? The answer must be multifactorial, but here are some of the component parts.

Freddie Gray had a number of potential causes for a failure to develop good executive functions. To begin at the beginning, his mother had used heroin during pregnancy, and substance abuse during pregnancy is a risk factor for the developing fetus. He was born prematurely, the product of a twin gestation delivered at 7 months of gestation: his condition at birth required weeks of care in a neonatal intensive care unit. Prematurity is a risk factor for delayed or impaired motor and cognitive development and for poor executive function later on. And once home, he was the victim of ongoing exposure to a brain toxin. Freddie had lead poisoning.

CHAPTER 3:

Baltimore and Freddie and Lead

Baltimore has had a long relationship with lead and, not coincidentally, with its various toxicities. We think of lead poisoning today primarily in connection with exposure to lead paints both in connection with painting the keels of boats – Falmouth, Mass. figured prominently in this problem in the 1950s and 1960s – and domestic painting in houses. Until its problems were recognized and it became illegal, lead was added to gasoline, where it improved the efficiency of combustion and acted as a lubricant to moving parts. Unfortunately, it also exposed workers and users to its poisonous side effects. Most recently, the exposure of lead contamination in drinking water, scandalously highlighted in Flint, Michigan, has come from the use of lead in service pipes, including those bearing water to houses. Lead was valued for its easy workability and long life, superior to materials previously used in pipes, paint, and other applications both industrial and domestic. And it was even valued as an additive for consumption: it found a use as a sweetening agent in wine, as far back as the Roman empire and as recently as the 18th century. A great deal of literature – observational, epidemiological, and experimental – supports the negative influence of lead on brain function generally. Exposure need not mean direct consumption. Benjamin Franklin, visiting London in 1724, observed the effects of working with lead in drying print type and other types of exposures, and described them at length, including his previous observations of toxicity associated with lead ingestion and exposures, in a letter of 1784. In between then and now, a number of authors described lead toxicity as "colic" and noted it as a cause of what we would today call peripheral neuropathy (what Franklin called "Dangles", because of the limp postures of limbs affected by lead-induced peripheral neuropathy). It was also a useful deliberate poison. Acute lead poisoning – resulting from the rapid accumulation of high levels of lead- is known to result in an encephalopathic picture which includes brain swelling, seizures, and even death, with residua for survivors of ongoing impairment of brain functioning. Acute lead poisoning has been primarily associated with workers in lead. It is also possible to acquire a significant lead burden by frequent exposure to a person who works with lead, through contamination with clothing, or through other exposures. What is less clear is the impact of the more gradual accumulation of lead in the body, and the levels at which "toxicity" occurs. Lead accumulation may even begin before birth. Lead is stored in bone and is mobilized during pregnancy. For the mother, it may cause gestational hypertension, pre-eclampsia and premature birth or abortion, and it is associated with adverse fetal outcomes (though not major malformations). It may cross the placenta and enter the developing fetus, accumulating in bones and other organs and crossing the blood-brain barrier to reach the brain. Although this problem is recognized by the American College of Obstetricians and Gynecologists, which in 2012 put the number of women of childbearing age with levels currently considered toxic at one per cent, routine screening of pregnant women or of newborns was not then and is not currently recommended in a position paper of 2018. Instead, risk factor assessment of individual patients – with the usual inaccuracies, delays, and omissions of history taking – is recommended, and then subsequent screening of those patients with any risk factor. Risk factors extend to cooking in, or using, lead-glazed ceramics, the use of certain cosmetics, or herbal medicines, eating non-food substances (pica) and the consumption of lead-contaminated water.

Lead poisoning is not a problem of the past, though the numbers are dropping. According to the Registry of lead poisoning cases in the Environmental Department of the State of Maryland, in Baltimore City in 2018 there were 383 cases in children, 2.4% of them new. And it was a problem for Freddie, who had been treated repeatedly – six or more times – for lead poisoning. The blood level of lead considered toxic is currently 5 ug/dL, but this is challenged as a normal upper limit, and no level is really considered safe. Court documents entered at the time of his mother's suit concerning the lead poisoning of her children state that Freddie's reached at least 37 ug/dL at the age of 2, and they remained elevated over an uncertain but extended period of time. This level would be expected to result in the compromise of brain functions. The medical literature referenced in the Entrez Pubmed website under the pertinent search headings reports that the presence of lead at any level is associated with the loss of cognitive and judgmental functions; with relative disinhibition, impulsiveness, poor judgment – collectively described as executive functions – and the loss of I.Q. points generally. Treatment aimed at removing lead from the body - called "chelation-" and altering diet to provide substances such as zinc to compete with lead, is usual once elevated levels are identified, but this does not result in reversal of all of its chronic effects on the brain. In the long run, the condition is best avoided by restrictions on lead-containing substances, from pipes to gas to paint, and lead avoidance and/or removal once contamination is identified. This is difficult to do if the lead is in the water you drink, the soil in which you garden, or the air you breathe. Also, of course, restrictions have to be enforced. Landlords are now obliged to remove lead from their properties, but have routinely failed to do so despite fines and lawsuits, and as usual a lively business has spring up to profit from the consequences. In 2008 Gray's family successfully sued their landlord, Stanley Rochkind, for the lead poisoning of the three children in the family who, like any number of others, became the recipients of "lead checks". This provision speaks to the recognition of the cognitive, and hence educational and employability handicaps, of the victims. But the provision of money does not fix the enduring negative effects of lead poisoning. And the recipients of lead checks in turn were preyed upon by persons equivalent to contemporary "same day loan" entrepreneurs. According to a *Washington Post* investigative report of 08/2018 by Terrence McCoy, Freddie sold the rights to future checks, worth a total of $94,000, for about $18,000. His sisters, also victims of lead poisoning, sold the rights for their checks worth $435,000 for $54,000. The buyer was Access Funding, which offers quick payouts to lead poisoning victims.

As they say: poor executive judgment.

CHAPTER 4:

Freddie Goes to School

If the streets shackled my right leg, the schools shackled my left. Ta-Nehisi Coates, *Between the World and Me.* Coates was born in 1975 and attended the Baltimore public schools.

Public Education in the city of Baltimore when Freddie, who would be a special class student in need of supportive services went to school, was, and is, a mess, though it has not always been so (and it may be currently improving). Periodically, it has even been regarded as a model, as when it first achieved school desegregation per Federal legislation passed in the wake of *Brown vs. Board of Education* in May of 1954. Four months later, Baltimore schools were desegregated as a matter of official policy when they opened. In fact, desegregation at some levels had been achieved long before that court decision. To read through Baltimore's history of public school education and educational desegregation – real or, as at present, largely imagined - is a polyphonic experience: the voices sing to different music, concurrently. What one hears from official publications is often a hymn of praise. What one hears from contemporary reports is often discordant. What one hears from black participants, looking back on their personal experiences after 60 years, is decidedly mixed.

Public education in general was a rarity nationwide, in consideration and in execution, until the late 18th century. Until that point education had been at the hands of tutors or, as it evolved, private schools for which a fee was paid. But by the first quarter of the 19th century, the public school movement was swelling in New York, Boston, and St. Louis. Early advocates of public education were Ecclesiasts, and their arguments and institutions were moral and charitable in intent, with a characteristically Protestant serving of self-interest. Appreciation of changing social conditions and the recognition of the association of education and social welfare was ably articulated. Rapid growth of the City of Baltimore had led to sequestration of the poor into neighborhoods where crime and "vagrancy" – what we would now call homelessness - were increasingly prevalent. The poor, of course, were overwhelmingly persons of color (including the now academically outstanding Asian population). As argued in the General Assembly, "Whether the child be of Indian or African, European or Asian descent; his ignorance will be a blight and his vice a curse to the community in which he lives". The first successful public Academy was established by Methodists in 1797 (an earlier Academy, launched in 1786, had lasted only 10 months). In 1826 a General School Law was passed which created a Board of Commissioners of Public Schools, "To establish and regulate a system of free public education". By 1828 the Commission was established, and the following year three schools were opened, with 269 pupils. Education was still largely the privilege of White children, though some schools for Blacks were established independently. By 1866 the position of State Superintendent of Public Instruction was created and filled by the Reverend John N. M'Jilton, a Methodist Episcopal pastor. Free primary schools and education for Negroes and the handicapped were proposed, as was compulsory education. The State of Maryland was more progressive than the individual Maryland Counties, however. Although local control of schools was shifted to State control, with modification of the distribution of State revenues so that taxes derived from Negroes were to be dedicated to Negro education, it was not until 1872 that free public education for Negroes was mandated. At that time control had been returned to County and District Commissioners, appointed by circuit court judges of the State. Although a number of schools had been assimilated into the public school system, the first High School for Negros – the Frederick Douglas High School, still in existence – was not established until 1882, and the first black teachers hired in 1889.

While this might be seen as progress, it also reinforced the pattern of demographic, hence racial, school segregation, and the founding principles of separate schooling remained in place until 1954 because of demographic factors (which endure to this day). Beginning in 1910 local legislation reinforced segregated housing patterns directly and segregated schooling indirectly. In that year the City of Baltimore enacted the first law in American history that prohibited Blacks from moving to white residential blocks and vice versa, according to Antero Peitila's book *Not in my Neighborhood*. In 1911, Councilman Samuel L. West authored an amended bill whereby block by block housing was designated as either Black or White. It read that no White person could move into a block in which more than half of the residents were colored, and vice-versa. Those who violated the law could be fined or face prison time. Baltimore became a national leader in racial segregation. Following Baltimore's lead, many other cities passed similar laws. Neighborhoods in Baltimore City like Roland Park, Guilford, Homeland and Northwood were some of the first planned suburban-like communities in America, designed to keep White residents from fleeing out of the city to the county suburbs. These neighborhoods became some of the earliest communities to bar African Americans by means of property deeds. The Baltimore Sun supported it, saying Baltimore would be on better legal footing if it "ostracized Blacks through binding private agreements instead of government legislation." Roland Park remains predominantly White today, with a 7 percent African American population. Homeland has an 8 percent Black population. Not much has changed since 1910: one block in Baltimore can be predominantly White and wealthy and another one block over can be poor and Black. Until 1962, the Federal Housing Authority (FHA) continued this legacy by promoting home ownership in new and primarily suburban neighborhoods so long as they were White and not ethically or economically diverse, effectively redlining (refusing a loan to a person because they live in an area deemed a financial risk: differentially refusing loans to Blacks). Jews were also excluded in these covenants. Generally lower property values in Black neighborhoods insured and continue to insure that those local schools would be supported by a lesser tax base. Because of poor schooling graduation rates declined and few went on to higher education (Coates himself, though he went to public schools, was from a middle-class Black background – his father was a publisher and a librarian – and he was admitted to Howard University, which he referred to as a Black Mecca for himself, and where he spent 5 years before leaving without graduating). But the students in Black neighborhoods were generally handicapped on multiple levels – socioeconomically, with all the implications of more crime, more drug use, greater health problems and less access to appropriate medical care, less parental stability and education.

———

By the 1930's educational change had been at least in the air, if not on the ground. In 1936 Thurgood Marshall, then the lawyer for the NAACP, successfully argued for the admission of a black student to the University of Maryland's law school. The argument was based on the absence of a comparable educational opportunity within the black school system, and was advanced with respect to other Graduate programs there throughout the 1930s and 40s. Moving subsequently to promote comparable opportunity in schools underpinning the way to higher education Marshall, working on behalf of the NAACP and the Baltimore Urban league, successfully brought a case against the Baltimore Polytechnic Institute in 1952. The Institute offered an outstanding A course, preparing students for admission to colleges of engineering in particular. It had refused admission to 16 black students who had applied. Challenges to such a policy rested on the Separate but Equal clause of the 14th Amendment. Baltimore schools were demonstrably, unarguably unequal in terms of structural, material and didactic resources. The alternative to admission was the expensive construction of a comparable facility for Blacks. The School Board caved: 15 black students entered. Although the majority of them subsequently failed to graduate – their prior preparation had been woefully inadequate – a number did graduate. And for a while, the Baltimore schools were regarded as a model of peaceful integration at multiple levels. A newspaper photograph from the Baltimore Sun in 1955 shows white protestors carrying signs, and a policeman, but the posture of the (sole) policeman shown is relaxed, and one feels that he is primarily there to direct marchers and prevent protestors from blocking street traffic, as well of course as to prevent anyone getting out of hand. The policeman carries a gun but it is a holstered pistol, and he wears no special protective gear. Nothing suggests violence, or an organized hate group. However, with the flight of more affluent persons and groups, largely white, to the suburbs, public schools deteriorated again into *de facto* segregated institutions, with the least support for schools in the most impoverished, and predominantly black, neighborhoods. Graduation rates declined and few went on to higher education. The pupils were often multiply handicapped. That was certainly the case with Freddie Gray, who grew up in an impoverished neighborhood with a heroin-addicted, functionally illiterate mother and no father in the house. In 2008, the year Freddie would have been 18, only a little over a third of students in the Baltimore city public schools graduated from high school. Unequal educational opportunity in such neighborhoods remains the case. A recent article by Talia Richman in the Baltimore Sun (June 17, 2019) reported the findings of an audit of Baltimore's public school vocational programs, to which special education students in particular are steered. As might be expected they were found to differ sharply by demographic areas, with the lowest performing schools, in predominantly Black neighborhoods, offering courses of meager content that did not prepare students for jobs that would raise them above the poverty level. Freddie, by the time he left George Washington Carver Vocational Technical School before finishing 9th grade, probably had at best the equivalent of a fifth or sixth grade education. As a student he was no doubt handicapped by his history of lead poisoning and his other environmental exposures. His reading comprehension was such that his charges, when he was in trouble with the law, had to be read and explained to him by his Bondsman. As quoted by Terrence McCoy in a Washington Post story of April 2015 Dr. Daniel Levy, a pediatrician at Johns Hopkins, said that "The fact that Mr. Gray had these high levels of lead (37

ug/dl) in all likelihood affected his ability to think and to self-regulate and pro-
foundly affected his cognitive ability to process information."

Freddie had made an attempt to straighten up. He had married, fathered a
child, divorced, and formed a relationship with a young woman who worked
as a personal care nurse. He wanted to have a child with her but she told him,
no, not until he got himself together. He went to a job placement center, may
or may not have followed up on 3 referrals, but was not hired – fewer than
10% of the 32,000 ex-offenders handled there since 2005 were successfully
placed. With little formal education, no real job skills, and a legacy of functionally impaired cognitive and organizational brain skills, he was not a prom-
ising candidate for legitimate employment. Other avenues would have opened
themselves. He smoked dope, and repeatedly got himself arrested for possession and sometimes more serious charges.

CHAPTER 5:

The Autopsy Report and the Charges

It was in the interests of the Baltimore Police Department, and certainly of the officers who would subsequently be charged, to establish that Gray had come to grief accidentally and in the van – not before, as a consequence of rough handling during the arrest, and not as a consequence of inappropriate custodial care at any point. This they largely accomplished by the great good luck of the acceptance of their story regarding the timing of the injury by the Forensic Pathologist, Dr. Carol Allan, and by the subsequent reliance of the Prosecuting Attorney Mosby on Allan's report. Although Allan did, in the autopsy report, distinguish police reporting and her conclusion about the timing of Gray's injury in a section carefully labelled OPINION, this was interpreted by Mosby, and by the media, as factual material derived from medical evidence. It wasn't. Additionally, and for reasons that are not entirely clear, Mosby embargoed the report itself from release. The rationale appears to have been the avoidance of contamination of any potential jury pool. Had it been directly seen, close reading by the media or anyone else who read it might have picked up on the distinction between medical fact and Allan's inferred opinion about the timing, which was entirely derived from the police. This was a tragic confusion. Sufficient attention to it, coupled with the clear evidence of the video of the arrest and the reports of witnesses, might have resulted in more appropriate charges being brought. Ultimately the report was leaked and largely reported, diffusing outward from the Baltimore Sun, but the distinction between opinion and medical fact was not reported by the Sun in its excerpts. Both Allan herself, and the Chief of the Department Dr. David Fowler, deserve criticism for letting the confusion stand.

To evaluate this flawed performance on the part of Allan, it is necessary to understand the job description of a forensic pathologist and its performance by her. That task consists in using evidence derived from physical examination of the body in question, and any pertinent laboratory evidence, to determine the cause or causes of injury and/or death. It may also, in the case of a forensic autopsy, involve circumstantial information gathering. The timing of the event in question may also be important, and can in some cases be inferred from a number of factors, but these factors are dependent upon circumstance and they have a highly variable margin of error. If a body is found, say, in the woods, and without rigor mortis, and if the night is freezing and the body warm, then death is reasonably inferred to have been recent – within the framework of a certain number of hours, depending on the relative temperatures and the warmth-retaining properties of any clothing involved. Of course, the body might have been kept in warming circumstances for some time after death, and then left in the woods, but in that case other clues would have been available, having to do with time-dependent physiological changes in organs and other tissues. The state of digestion of stomach contents might provide a time frame in which the last meal was taken, for example: presumably, the person would have been alive at that time. If, on the other hand, a partially decomposed body is found, the state of decomposition and the colonization by attendant organisms provide guides to timing. Bugs, it turns out, are highly selective: different ones show up at different times. Such changes take place over hours and days, even longer. They cannot fix a time within a 45 minute van ride, especially 8 days after the event. In any case, there were no bugs at that point. There may be many other clues available, depending on the circumstance, but *in Gray's case there would have been no evidence from an autopsy or laboratory examination whatsoever that could fix the time of injury or death in the 45 minute interval of Gray's van ride.* (Allan did know this, and did not make

such a claim in her autopsy report: in her testimony to the court, she specifically rebutted the suggestion). This is particularly true if, as in this case, the
time interval in question is very short, and if autopsy examination takes place
over a week after the event, after extensive manipulation or other treatment.
In Gray's case, manipulation included not only the handling at the time of
transport to the hospital but also included both an attempt, first, at a "closed'
reduction of his neck fracture – that is, attempted reduction by external manipulation, such as traction – and then subsequent operative stabilization, as
well as the administration of drugs meant to modulate physiological changes.
It is also not possible to definitively infer a functional state at the time of injury
from autopsy examination, over a week after an event, from the state of tissues
in a case like Gray's when there has been extensive further manipulation or
other treatment aimed at interference with natural processes. Hence Allan's
inference of the timing of his injury and its consequences was entirely taken
from the history provided to her from the police. Allan did, in trial testimony,
distinguish between the primary and the secondary changes seen at autopsy:
as is well recognized, after an injury secondary changes take place which include swelling and cell death. These worsen the consequences of the original
injury and its clinical manifestations.

Allan talked to Col. Green; Lt. Norris; Major Frankfort, Lt. Kagan, and de-
tectives Teal and Austin, all of the BPD. They represented an investigative in-
terface between the pathologist and, by extension, with the Prosecution as
would be determined by Attorney Marilyn Mosby who was awaiting the autopsy report before bringing charges. Although Allan stated that she had also
reviewed the available videos of Gray's arrest, she testified in the trial of Officer
Rice that they did not offer her either the videos of the arrest or the witness
statements, all of which would have affirmed Gray's injury as occurring during the arrest and prior to being placed in the van. She herself had had no
training in clinical medicine, let alone neurology or neurosurgery, beyond
what she may have learned in medical school. She did not review the videos
with the expert neurosurgical witness for the prosecution, Dr. Soriano, prior
to releasing her report. She did not directly review the arrest video with any

other neurologically trained person. And ironically, because the charges were framed as they were, it was Joe Murtha, a defense lawyer for Porter, who did the most to undermine the assumption of timing in the autopsy report and thereby, by implication, placed the timing of the injury to the arrest process. In the trial Murtha, examining Allan, consistently pointed out that testimony from the police had determined Allan's sense of the timing, not physical or laboratory evidence. Curiously, her performance on the witness stand was more plausible than the report. She was a convincingly honest witness. As such, Allan acknowledged time after time that what she was referring to as "evidence" was not only laboratory and physical evidence, but a co-mingling of police testimony and true autopsy findings. The media covering the trial never picked upon that.

On the morning of April 20th, the day after Gray was officially declared dead and it was determined that the Gray case would demand a forensic autopsy, the Baltimore Police were already there to give her their version of the timing of events. Here is her testimony during a trial:

Attorney Murtha: *"So, on the 20th what did you actually do?"*

Allan: *"We review the forensic investigator's report based on the information that is given to him...I also had a substantial presence by the Baltimore City Police, and, as we discussed the particulars of a particular death, they offer information...I had a lot of information from the investigating agency."*

THE INVESTIGATING AGENCY REFERRED TO IS THAT OF THE BALTIMORE POLICE.

Murtha: *"And, in your examination you had made the determination that the cervical spine injury that you testified to, did not occur prior to (Gray's) entering into the police wagon, is that correct?"*

Allan: *"That is correct."*

This piece of testimony is sufficient to establish that Allan had not done an examination of the body before declaring the timing of the injury as occurring during the van ride. Unfortunately, however, Murtha used the word "examination" to refer to the basis of such a statement. He was referring to the "examination" of the circumstances as provided by the Police, not the autopsy itself. It thus again became confounded with medical and laboratory – actual autopsy – evidence. And this reiterated error persisted in the minds of the prosecuting attorneys and the media, and the public at large. The exchange establishes that the influence of police testimony was sufficient to lead Allan to accept the offered timing, despite the clear evidence of the arrest video that shows otherwise. Her pronouncement of the timing was out before the publication of the autopsy report, and it had devastating effects. Because it came from the Medical Examiner, it was assumed to have been derived from Medical Evidence. This was immediately accepted by the media, and effectively shut down further journalistic investigative efforts with regard to this vital aspect of the event.

The autopsy report also, by concluding that the cause of death was a homicide brought about by *omission* (failure to fasten the passenger securely with a seat belt; failure to obtain medical help for the passenger when he asked for it) rather than by *commission*, reinforced the conclusion that the injury had occurred in the van. It diverted attention from the arresting officers, who were in fact responsible initially for the injury that led to Gray's death.

Given the inescapable nightly videos of Gray's arrest which recorded his screams of agony, his publicized complaint of being unable to breathe, his legs obviously functionally useless from the rapidly evolving paralysis of his already broken neck as he is dragged to the van, why did Allan take a version of the history from the Police? In Expert Witness testimony of the trial on 12/9/15, Dr. Vincent DiMaio, a retired forensic pathologist, spoke as follows. **Note the sequencing:**

DiMiao:

*"A forensic autopsy consists of essentially 3 things – 1) a determination of the manner and circumstances surrounding the death, **now that may involve police investigative reports**, medical records – actually both of which were involved in this case; 2) **then** you do the physical autopsy, and 3) And then you do certain studies…So, you have all these things, and then you put them together and you issue a report as to the cause of death which is what killed the individual, and the manner of death, how it came about – accident, suicide, homicide, natural, undetermined."*

There was also the influence of Allan's supervisor, Dr. David Fowler. Fowler was (and is) the Chief Medical Examiner of the State of Maryland for the City of Baltimore, a well-known and respected person in the field. Fowler had authored, among other writings, a textbook of *Essential Forensic Neuropathology*. The text begins with instruction on the Gathering of Evidence, and indeed it recommends talking to the police. However, the entire construct offered by Fowler is that of a Forensic Pathologist (or Death Investigator) arriving at the scene of a newly discovered body: it is a yellow-tape scene, a scene newly controlled by the police. In this circumstance, Fowler writes, *"The time spent waiting to enter the controlled area around the body should be used to gather basic information from the police …and any available witnesses. If possible, information should include…How the body was discovered, Events surrounding the death, Medical history, and Social and mental history."* But this is a crime scene investigation scenario and not one applicable to the forensic autopsy examination of a brain-dead patient who died in a hospital bed. Fowler's book does not suggest uncritically taking and accepting information with regard to the timing of events from obviously self-interested parties, especially ones as notorious as the Baltimore Police. It did suggest interviewing witnesses, which Allan however did not do and did not regard as a part of her job (per her own subsequent testimony). One may infer from Fowler's book that the witnesses to be interviewed are there, on the spot, along with the police and a medical examiner called to the scene of discovery. The recommendation does not extend to advocating speculation about the circumstances of causality, or any aspect of the case that is not supported by physical or laboratory evidence. Such "evidence" has no place in an autopsy report.

The real question is why Allan ever accepted the account, given the reputation of the Baltimore Police for corruption and self-serving mendacity. Although gathering "circumstantial" accounts is recommended by both the National Association of Medical Examiner's (NAME) position paper and Fowler's book, there is also an admonishment to evaluate the veracity of such reports. It is unclear why Allan discounted the obvious evidence of the video of Gray's arrest, and why she accepted the descriptive term "combative" (which would be contradicted in later testimony by one of the Officers involved) or the description of Gray walking to the van or standing independently, or "entering" it. Instead he was shoved and dragged in, propped up and then left on his belly. That position was conflictingly described by officers Nero and Miller, but verified by Officer Rice and eye-witnesses. It is true that Allan had received no clinical training in medicine, let alone neurology, beyond what she might have learned as a medical student. It is possible that at the time of writing her report she did not realize that not all function has to disappear immediately, even given an injury which will eventually prove devastating. In her trial testimony, some months after the release of her report, she testified to the latter. Conceivably at the time of her report she accepted the thesis that Gray would have immediately lost all function after his original injury. However, the idea that after arrest he was feigning an inability to walk, and also that he really did "walk" and stand, bearing weight, independently, came entirely from the police. Allan acknowledged this as opinion, not evidence. No video record exists supporting this, despite subsequent interpretative claims to the contrary. On the contrary, the video reflects his facial expression of dazed agony and his failed attempt at supporting weight on one leg when an arresting officer audibly commands him to "WALK" as they drag him to the van, - shove him in when he visibly collapses at the van because he cannot enter it voluntarily - and leave him on his belly, face down and unsecured. As they drag him along to the van his head is seen to be cocked to the left, consistent with his already broken neck and the jumped facet joints which made turning it impossible. That point seems to have gone unnoticed by anyone, at least in the publicly recorded sphere.

———

As Chief of the Laboratory, Fowler signed off on Allan's final autopsy report, which references the timing provided by the police. Fowler should be censored for having allowed such a report to leave his office.

Because Allan gave her opinion of homicide to Mosby prior to release of the autopsy report, Mosby incorporated both that and Allan's opinion about the timing of the event into her charges. Her charges referenced the report: *"The findings of our comprehensive, thorough and independent investigation, coupled with the medical examiner's determination that Mr. Gray's death was a homicide that we received today, has led us to believe that we have probable cause to file criminal charges…the manner of death deemed homicide by the Maryland Medical Examiner is believed to be the result of a fatal injury that occurred while Mr. Gray was unrestrained by a seatbelt in the custody of the Baltimore Police Department Wagon.".* The timeline which she went on to present was entirely taken from the police reporting as it appeared in the Forensic report. And although Mosby refers to her "independent" investigation, it was coupled with investigation conducted by the police and taken from police reporting. Mosby: *"We leveraged the information made available by the police department".* The reference "independent investigation" seemed to largely consist of sending people to look for witnesses, and knocking on doors of unoccupied houses. As Prosecutor Bledsoe said, people in Freddie's neighborhood don't like to talk to officials. But some witnesses, per their statements to reporters, were never called upon, and some, easily identified on video, were never called to trial, though they had information to offer. Harold Perry, who told reporters that he heard Gray screaming in pain and pleading "Get off my neck", was one of them; Alethea Booze was another. But what they had to say would have placed the timing of Gray's injury before the van ride. And that would have been contrary to the charges as brought. But they were there: they saw it happen.

The timeline presented in Mosby's statement of charges was thereafter widely accepted by the media, which interpreted it as being based on "medical evidence".

Mosby, after all, had indicated that she had consulted the forensic pathologist when she announced the charges on May 1. *But there was no pertinent medical evidence to support that timing.* Even assuming, for the moment, that the injury happened in the van, it would not have been possible to determine from autopsy evidence the moment or minutes in which the fracture occurred during the 45 minute interval between arrest and the last van stop. From that point on, however, the media consistently referred to " Freddie Gray, who was injured during a van ride".

The media actually had a lot to answer for. The National Networks and even NPR, with their tiresome endless reiterations about their superior fact-checking of every story, accepted and amplified the SUFFERED AN INJURY IN THE VAN story. Late in the case Jennifer Ludden, the NPR reporter, got some of the NPR broadcasters to start saying at least occasionally that Gray was "injured while in police custody" instead, and occasionally the *NY Times* and a network broadcast would phrase it that way also, but it was too far along to make any difference in the generality of public perception. Although the media complained about the judicial restrictions on their access to testimony and witnesses, and the fact that none of the Baltimore neurosurgeons would talk to them, they would not have had to go far afield to learn that fixing the timing of Gray's injury on the basis of "medical evidence" was not possible. A phone call to a pathologist at any hospital would have done it. A little research on the timing of the clinical manifestations of spinal cord injury would have done it. Reviewing the arrest video with an outside neurosurgeon would have done it. There were instead frequent references to the assumed ability of the medical evidence to exactly fix the timing of the injury: for example, a guest on Anderson Cooper (CNN) thus commented, without challenge or correction. (When corrected in correspondence by a physician, there was no response from Cooper or CNN). Cooper had initially seemed to believe the evidence of his own eyes on seeing the video, but he soon gave up. He had also, in April 2015, interviewed a relative of a BPD officer who said that that person believed that the arresting officers had broken his neck. Why this courageous statement was never further pursued is inexplicable.

Allan's assessment of the timing when Mosby announced her charges had not been based on any medical evidence, nor were they said to be in the autopsy report. Even in the autopsy report itself, Allan used the words "by report" or "reportedly" some 8 times, and always the reference is understood to be the reporting of the police. Sadly, even Wikipedia currently says that "The medical evidence found that Gray had sustained the injuries while in transport". *There was no such medical evidence: the statement concerning timing in the autopsy report was based on what the police had said.* And both then and in the subsequent official autopsy report, statements by eyewitnesses to the arrest were omitted, though a number of such witnesses were readily identifiable on the video and included of course Kevin Moore, who shot the video. Here and there some contrary opinion about the timing peeked through, either in letters to the Editor in various papers or in one article by Sheryl Stolberg and Jess Bidgood in the *New York Times*. Nonetheless, because Allan was the identified forensic pathologist, the police version of the timing became imbued with medical authority. Most importantly, Mosby in particular referred to taking the timing from the Medical Examiner. In announcing the charges against the police officers, Mosby stated specifically that the fatal insult had occurred inside the van, and not before, and indicated that she had spoken to Allan. The subsequent issuance of her charges all referred to that timing, which in turn meant that there was no direct evidence of the event that could be offered. Unfortunately for verification, vans do not have cameras. This was a critical error. There were no visual witnesses to what happened *in* the van, in contrast to the number of witnesses present at the arrest, and the video evidence shot at that time. There was no video evidence shot inside the van. By accepting the timing offered by Allan and the police, the charges were converted to occurring, unprovably, during a time frame that obliterated video and eye-witness evidence. The Forensic definition of homicide, according to NAME, is not the same thing as a legal definition of homicide, which varies from State to State. Despite the ME determination of homicide, if it happened in the van it was arguably an accident or just custodial carelessness, albeit in defiance of a recently articulated Departmental Policy *re* securing passengers during transport. Which was what the police wanted.

At a later time, Baltimore journalist Ericka Blount interviewed the Executive Director of the Department of Public Safety Russell Neverdon. He told her: "They are using terms like 'failure' and 'negligence' – terms associated with a civil case. Not a criminal case.'" It was a stroke of unbelievably good fortune for the police.

CHAPTER 6:

Constructing the Charges and the Defense

On May 1, 2015, Baltimore City State Attorney General Marilyn Mosby had announced the charges against the arresting officers. Six officers were charged: arresting officers Edward Nero and Garrett Miller; Lt. Brian Rice, who had initiated the arrest and who as the Senior Officer was technically in charge; officer Caesar Goodson, the driver of the van, and officers William Porter and Alicia White who responded to post-arrest calls for assistance. White had already been called to investigate a citizen witness complaint of inappropriate police handling of Gray, so going to the scene was a two-fer for her. Variably distributed charges were Involuntary Manslaughter (Porter, Rice, White); Assault in the Second Degree: Intentional, or Negligent, depending (Goodson, Nero, Miller, Porter, Rice, White); Reckless Endangerment (Porter), Second Degree Depraved Heart Murder (Goodson); Vehicular Manslaughter (Goodson); False Imprisonment (Miller, Nero, Rice), and Misconduct in Office (everybody). The most serious charge brought, that of Depraved Heart Murder, was directed at Goodson, the van driver, in conformity with the long Baltimore Police Department history of deliberately rough van rides. A traditional excuse for van rides resulting in injury to the prisoner was that the van had been deliberately swayed or stopped abruptly – repeatedly – to avoid a dog. Or dogs. This got to be such a patently tired explanation that the then Commissioner of Police, Batts, had admonished van drivers that if they wanted to go on claiming that that was the reason, they had better come with the dog. (Other Commissioners, in other venues, had apparently said so as well). The least serious charge was that of Misconduct in Office: bad as it sounds, it is a civil, not a criminal, offense.

A BPD history, with documentation stretching back to 1980, of broken necks ascribed to accidents (or deliberately rough rides) in the van, oddly offered both the police a fall-back position and Mosby a lead-in to the charges brought. The police appreciated it because they could maintain that some untoward accident or even a deliberately self-injurious act on the part of the prisoner had happened in the van, as they had successfully maintained with regard to the previous incidents. Accepting a correspondence to the history of 3 previous cases of necks found broken after transport might place a similar incident in the category of at worst an accident ascribable to careless neglect of a new directive, issued shortly before the Gray incident – a requirement that all prisoners in a van be seat-belted. Thus, by retrospectively reporting prior cases a month before the charges were announced and also again 16 months later on the previous incidents, the Baltimore Sun may have inadvertently done the police a favor. It raised the previous incidents, and relatively exculpatory judgments, in everyone's consciousness. It certainly didn't bring the Gray case up to the "Well-What's- the- Big- Deal- This-Happens- all- the- Time" level, but it perhaps didn't hurt as much as it should have either. For the prosecution, it also provided a dance-step to the alleged timing of Gray's injury and, helped to place it in the transport process, thus avoiding the uncomfortable situation of a black prosecutor directly charging the arresting officers, all of whom were white, with the most serious charges (to which they were fully entitled). We cannot know Mosby's level of consciousness about that at the time: hence speculation about her motive would be unfair.

The Forensic Medical Pathologist had declared Gray's broken neck a homicide, and Mosby followed suit, satisfying the public perception and her own determination to illustrate that Black Lives Matter. And although homicide is popularly understood to imply a deliberate act, forensically and legally it need not be intentional. Forensic and legal definitions of homicide are not equivalent. Legally, the definition of homicide depends on where you live. But even if you live where the homicide is homicide, intentional or not, it's better that it be clearly unintentional. The penalties are less.

The distinction between declaring a death an accident or a homicide has been outlined by a position paper by the National Association of Medical Examiners (NAME), with regard to REPORTING OF DEATHS IN CUSTODY. Oddly, the legal definition of Homicide differs from State to State, and turns upon the distinction between the foreseeable or unforeseeable predictability of causing fear, harm or death. If someone dies because of a foreseeable consequence of an act, that is a legal Homicide in Maryland. However, in Texas a classical hunting accident would be an "Accidental" death, if fatal, whereas in Maryland it would be a Homicide: even if the shooter were aiming at a deer, and missed and killed another person, that would be a Homicide. Firing a gun at a live target in any circumstance foreseeably results in a harm: it need not be pre-meditated with regard to the person shot. The Prosecution would argue that failure to follow the Departmental Directive to seat-belt all passengers could be foreseen to potentially cause harm. The Defense would argue that in practice nobody usually seat-belted prisoners anyway, which seems an odd defense, but still. Defense would hope that any charge more serious than "Accidental" would be based on circumstantial evidence, since there were no cameras or eye-witnesses inside the van, and thus it might be dismissable. So with regard to precedent, the Baltimore Sun probably did the police a favor by reporting on the previous instances of broken necks ascribed to accidents inside a police van. A Directive to seatbelt all passengers had not been issued, at the time of the previous injuries.

These were the previous incidents **of record:** The earliest reported incident occurred in 1980. In that year a 58 year old man named John Wheatfall was arrested in mid-afternoon for drunk and disorderly conduct. We have no details about the way in which he was handled during the arrest, but his family said that he was normally neat and respectably dressed, and that his clothes after the arrest were dirty and torn. They inferred rough handling. He was taken to the police station in a van. When the officers couldn't get him to move himself out of the van, they lugged him into the station. When an hour later he still wasn't moving he was transported to St. Agnes hospital, where he was found to have a broken neck. The police "investigated" and said that nobody had been found to do anything wrong. The family disagreed with them and sued. The judge disagreed with the family concerning the charge of negligence. The jury however awarded them what was then the maximum allowable amount for an accidental injury - $20,000. We were unable to ascertain his time of death: there seems to have been no obituary, at least in the Baltimore Sun.

The next case occurred in 1997. Jeffrey Alston, 32, was stopped for speeding, failed a breathalyzer test, was arrested for drunk driving and transported in a van to jail. Allegedly, although handcuffed, he got himself out of the handcuffs and undid his also alleged seatbelt. Not once, but twice. He allegedly thrashed about and allegedly kept ramming his head into the sides of the van and the plastic window in front of the van, thereby, allegedly, breaking his own neck. He was taken to Sinai Hospital when the van was opened again and he complained of "feeling numb" and, *like Freddie Gray, he complained of difficulty breathing.* At Sinai he was found to have a broken neck. He told his doctors that the police had put him in a headlock hold and tossed him face down into the van, where he helplessly rolled around in a rough ride. Remarkably, the examining trauma surgeon at Sinai found no external signs of head trauma from the alleged self-battering. The jury awarded him 39 million dollars, the price of a broken neck apparently having gone up, but he settled for 6 million. A life-long paraplegic, he died in 2008. No autopsy report was available.

The third recorded victim of a broken neck was a 62 year old man, Dondi Johnson, who was arrested in 2005 for public urination, transported in a van, and emerged from it with a broken neck. He died 2 weeks later from the consequences of his injury: although the immediate cause was listed as pneumonia, this is a frequent accompaniment of the immobility and lung stasis from such an injury. Before he died he described being cuffed but not belted in a van, and an aggressively rough ride that tossed him helplessly about on the floor. Johnson was awarded 7.4 million, but this was reduced to $219,000, the maximum possible after a new Maryland State law capping awards. These careless accidents were getting awfully expensive for the police. No autopsy report was available.

So the precedent of blaming an accident in the van for a broken neck was well-established, and may have been partly true. Intent was not provable, nor was foreseeability of harm. (Rough rides were not unique to Baltimore: similar reports came from a number of such events in major cities -Albuquerque, Chicago, Philadelphia, San Francisco). The element of deliberate rough rides was denied, of course, and at least two of the three previous injuries probably took place before the van ride, but the unsecured rides in the van may certainly have made the spinal injuries caused by initial cervical fractures worse by moving unstable fragments of bone or cartilage. As Dr. J-J. Gunning, the Medical Director at St. Agnes, was quoted as saying with regard to John Wheatfall: "A person with a broken neck does not always become paralyzed…Whether paralysis ensues depends on many different things, including the severity of the fracture…moving a person who has such a break 'conceivably' could aggravate the injury."

For sure.

The charges, as they were brought, must have made the police and their defense team very happy. False imprisonment (which may be only unreasonable detainment) was almost laughable – the police had been getting away with that for years. So-called Terry stops were easily defended by invoking the Supreme Court rulings in Terry v. Ohio (1968) and Illinois v. Wardlow (2000), its even more police-friendly Supreme Court decision. In any case, Freddie never made it to jail. So he wasn't exactly literally imprisoned: he died first. Misconduct in Office was only a civil offense. The most serious charges of Depraved Heart Murder and Vehicular Manslaughter would need to establish a deliberate rough ride by Goodson, but he was not known for that and no one could come up with previous charges to establish a reputation as far as he was concerned.

That wouldn't have been allowed by the Judge in any case. Vehicular man-slaughter makes it sound like he had run Freddie Gray over with a vehicle, or deliberately used one to hurt him in some other way. Intent is hard to prove. Additionally, he was the only officer to suggest – twice – that Gray needed to be taken for medical attention rather than directly to Central Booking. Reck-less endangerment rested on the failure to seatbelt Gray, but the defense would be that nobody did that anyway, Policy or no Policy. This was for reasons of officer safety, supposedly: getting close enough to a prisoner to fasten the seat-belt might have been dangerous for the officer, even if the prisoner were hand-cuffed. The various assault charges were another matter, but they were mostly based on the seatbelt issue anyway and they could deal with that. Police inves-tigating Police. Records could get lost. Rationales could be manufactured.

Before the charges had been brought, Officer Novak, an original investigating officer who had also been part of the team that dragged Gray along to the van, had texted to the officers charged: "I'll help you guys in any way I can." *An in-vestigating officer promises to help the alleged perps: "I'll help you guys in any way I can."* Miller, an arresting Officer who in the Kevin Moore video can be seen kneeling on Gray's neck, had tweeted "Well we are all fucked." As well they might have been, but they weren't.

Oddly, although the other cell phone conversations between the officers had had been subpoenaed by the Prosecution, the police failed to deliver the sub-poenas in a timely fashion, so they expired. Those conversations were not heard. The brotherhood had closed ranks. The fix was in.

CHAPTER 7:

When Did They Really Break His Neck?

SOME STATEMENTS FROM PHYSICIANS:

"I am a neurologist and I too noticed that he was paralyzed prior to being placed in the van. Has AAN released a statement on this? I want to help in any way I can." – Kita Williams, MD Assistant Professor, Dept. of Neurology, The Vanderbilt Clinic, Nashville, TN

"In the video showing Gray being dragged into the police van, his legs appear to be flaccid. It's entirely possible that his neck was broken by the police before he was placed in the van, i.e. in taking him to the ground and/or restraining him there; I have seen similar opinions expressed online by other physicians. Yet in the recent acquittal of the police van driver, it was assumed by the court that his neck was broken inside the transport van." –Alan Meyers, MD, MPH Professor of Pediatrics (recently retired) Boston University school of Medicine.

"To whom it may concern: In reviewing the Moore video it is my professional opinion that spinal cord injury signs were present prior to Mr. Gray's being placed in the van. I would be willing to elaborate further if you wish to contact me." –Alexander G Reeves Md Professor and Chair Emeritus, Section of Neurology Dartmouth-Hitchcock Medical Center. From a letter to Mosby.

State Attorney for Baltimore City Mosby, who brought the charges, had at her disposal any number of statements from physicians contradicting her assumption concerning the timing of Gray's injury and the charges flowing from that assumption. A letter to the American Academy of Neurology listserve urging concerned physicians to write to her produced responses: we do not know how many, exactly, and we are not going to be allowed to find out. But no matter how many were written, they were reactive to what had already been done. It was unfortunately too late to correct and reverse, or amend, the charges that already had been laid. Instead, a form letter was generated. Mine is identical to others received, but it was sent in response to a communication that had preceded her announcement of the charges.

The ultimate declaration of the timing of Gray's injury had rested on three things: in the first instance, on the testimony of Police, which contradicted the testimony of the witnesses and the video of the arrest. In the second instance, it rested on the mistaken popular belief that a "broken neck" would have led to immediate paralysis and inability to speak or even breathe. And in the third instance, it depended on Allan's testimony that Gray's fractured neck could only have occurred, given that it happened in the van, by Gray somehow arising and then falling in such a way as to break his own neck by his own actions. None of these assumptions hold up to informed scrutiny.

With regard to accepting the testimony of the police concerning the timing of the incident – and the supposedly benign nature of the arrest - this in essence cleared the arresting officers of direct responsibility, and transformed the event into an unfortunate accident, albeit an accident related to negligence in securing his safety and a violation of official police policy. But Defense Attorney Murtha established that there was no true *medical* evidence to support the timing of the injury, and there was no other evidence either. That timing was contradicted by the eyewitnesses who were never called at the trial, and the video evidence. Not all of the eye-witnesses were believable – two of them said that Gray had been tazed, one, that he had been beaten – but all confirmed that Gray had been injured before he had to be dragged to the van. Accepting the Police version was an obvious and inexcusable error on the part of the Baltimore and State Office of the Medical Examiner and, specifically, the assigned examiner, Carol Allan MD and her responsible supervisor, David Fowler MD. Ample documentation already existed of the need for the independent investigation of incidents of harm occurring in police custody in general – that was what the Citizen Review Board was supposed to be about - and above all, in an instance where a notably corrupt and mendacious police force might have to implicate themselves or members of their fellow officers.

The second set of assumptions concerning the implications of a broken neck, however, require some unraveling. Coupled with the Police narrative, they underpinned the fiction of the timing.

———

A broken neck is not any one thing, though it is commonly referred to as though it were. In medical terms, a broken neck refers only to fracturing of the bony spinal vertebrae. It is possible to have a broken neck without any neurological deficit at all. Accompanying such a fracture, there is often (but not inevitably) fracture or displacement of the cartilaginous discs between the vertebrae, and spinal cord injury resulting from their displacement and subsequent compression, or contusion, of the spinal cord. The spinal cord runs like a heavily trafficked highway through the protective tunnel created by the bony vertebrae of the spine. The vertebrae are what you feel if you run your hand down the middle of someone's back. There are usually 33 of them: seven protecting the spinal cord in the neck, 12 in the thorax or mid-body, five in the lumbar region, 5 in the sacrum and 3- 5 in the coccyx. Down to the sacral area, the vertebrae are cushioned and spaced out by cartilaginous discs between them; The lower vertebrae are fused to each other, and attached to the pelvis. The spinal cord does not run through them, but descending nerve roots from the cord do – they are called the *cauda equina*, or horse's tail, from their appearance – and these roots exit through the sacral vertebral exit holes (foramina). The intervertebral discs between the lumbar vertebrae are the ones that cause the most routine trouble, especially as we age, by occasionally breaking off fragments that cause pain and /or muscle weakness by pressing on the nerves as they exit the cord through the "exit" openings in the bony spine. If you live long enough you will probably at some point have a problem with them, even if you didn't have an accident or some other direct trauma.

The spinal cord, and the nerve pathways that exit from it and enter into it, carries all of the information transmitted to and from the brain about what to do and how to do it. It sends out connections to other nerves and muscles, tissues and other organs, transmitting its information by generating tiny electrical messages. A good deal of this information is consciously perceived, but a lot is not: the autonomic nervous system fibers in the cord, for example, tell you to breathe without conscious instruction (although you can consciously suspend that instruction, by willfully holding your breath). The spinal cord also carries information back to the brain – pain, temperature, and so forth. And, remarkably, the spinal cord has built-in reflexes telling it what to do in certain situations, without waiting to carry it back to the brain and get instructions. The spinal cord doesn't always wait for you to feel something and figure out what to do about it: it already knows. Even before birth it develops sufficiently – from built-in, genetically programmed memory – to carry information about what to do in the future. Babies too young to walk, when held above a table and then positioned so that the top of their foot is drawn across the edge of it, will make a primitive stepping motion – the so-called stepping and placing reflex, present, remarkably, even weeks before a term baby is born. It largely disappears when the baby matures enough to actually be walking. The gag reflex, however, occurring involuntarily in response to a noxious stimulus (which can be physical or psychological or both), remains indefinitely.

The spinal cord and its nerves can be injured by penetration of a foreign object – a knife, or bullet fragment, for example. Or they can be injured by bony overgrowth - arthritic changes, essentially, that come with age – or by fragments of the spinal vertebrae, or cartilaginous fragments of discs, pressing on the cord or its exiting nerves and thereby impeding its function. "Broken" necks are characterized by bony fractures of the vertebrae, and they can result in varying degrees of compression of the cord, but that comes in degrees of resultant injury. It is possible to have a vertebral fracture that does no actual damage, though almost always it is painful. Whatever the cause and whatever the degree, the first rule in neck injury is to stabilize, by immobilization, the injured neck. The movement of unstable fragments of bone or disc may cause resultant injury to the cord. It is unprovable, but entirely possible, that being hauled in and out of the van multiple times, and dragged, per Porter's testimony, to a semi-upright position leaning against the van bench at stop 4, worsened the consequences of his already broken neck.

Attributing the timing of injury to the van ride depended on the incorrect assumption that *all* function would immediately cease below the level of a broken neck which had resulted in damage to the spinal cord. **This is not correct.** When injury to the spinal cord does occur, the initial manifestations of injury may not fully reflect the ultimate damage done. *This is a critical point to understand.* The effects of spinal cord injury and its ultimate consequences are not necessarily immediately and fully evident. The ultimate effects of spinal cord injury evolve, with variable time courses. For one thing, certain capacities, and their resultant activity, are either pre-programmed or stored in the cord at various levels. An example familiar to all is that of what are called nociceptive reflexes. The word is derived from the Latin verb *nocere*, meaning to hurt. Hurt in turn may refer to pain, or physical harm, or both, because of course they are closely linked. If you step on a tack, say, or stick your foot into bathwater that is too hot, the foot is jerked back and withdrawn immediately, and this happens even before the pain is consciously felt. The painful sensation did not need to make its way up the spinal cord, into the brain, await perceived consciousness of injury, and then receive a command from the brain which then must travel down the spinal cord and have the upper motor neurons tell the lower motor neurons to tell the nerves to tell the muscles to pull the foot away: there is a pre-programmed, and usefully protective, local reflex arc which takes care of that, fast. (Subsequently, the brain may process the event, and even usefully store it in memory, for future reference: "Ouch, that hurt!!" ("*Well,* *next time, watch where you're going. Or check the water temperature first. How many times do I have to tell you this?")* Because some reflexes develop even before birth, not all motor activity depends upon an intact or fully mature spinal cord. Premature babies – even as young as 28 weeks of gestation – have a number of automatic reflexes. Some, such as sucking or swallowing, are there ready for use. At six months of gestation, babies photographed in utero may be seen sucking their thumbs! Grimacing in response to a needle prick on the cheek and other movements initiated by various stimuli, take place. Some reflexes and motor acts are lodged above the level of the spinal cord, processing information from the eyes and ears. Other reflexes, however, short-circuit the spinal cord pathways that reach the brain from below and, like the nociceptive reflex described above, do not depend upon spinal cord activity descending from the neck. They depend, initially, on information stored in local arcs below the level of descending information. Among these reflexes are the automatic stepping and placing reflexes which can be elicited in newborns. The baby can't walk, of course - the necessary motor strength is not yet developed – but the appropriate gestures and postural reflexes are there already.

With maturity, motor strength, coordination and subsequent motor memory develop. Motor memory is an interesting phenomenon - part reflex, part brain-determined, and all of it muscle-dependent. When we walk -indeed, when any animal locomotes – it is not necessary to think about, or command, every individual step. As long as no special situation arises – such as the need for careful footing when crossing a narrow bridge, for example – the motor act is automatic. You don't have to think about, or look to verify, each step. If you are practicing a new dance sequence, you at first need to think about what goes where when, but then it becomes part of an automatically programmed sequence initiated by other cues. Or, if you climb a ladder for a first time, you probably look at where you place your foot for the next step. After a few experiences, you don't need to look, if it's the same ladder – your motor memory already knows what to do. Moreover, motor memory can be stored with information related to not only how, but how long. If you are a regular walker of a habitual distance - for example, if you always walk your dog for a certain distance on your nightly stroll - you may have had the experience of walking along an unfamiliar route for a change, or in some other circumstance. After your usual distance, your steps slow and you are ready to turn around. This is not a function of fatigue – after all, you usually walked back – but it is a function of motor memory. Motor, i.e. muscle, memory, coupled with spinal reflex activity, is why chickens can briefly run with their heads cut off (that's not just a saying, it's a fact). The muscle memory for attempted running away in any menacing situation, for which being picked up, restrained, and placed, neck extended, on a bloody chopping block would reasonably qualify, is already there for the chicken. So, menaced, it runs, even without its head which houses the brain which would normally tell the spinal cord to tell the legs to run. The chicken can still run, for a little while. The muscles and nerves empowering that have not yet processed being deprived of the normal regulatory and nutritional support from above. They have some functional reserve.

Little discussed by physicians, but well-recognized especially by neurologists, is the astonishing fact that movement of the human body can take place even after death. These movements – usually head turning, rigid semi-upright posturing, or arm flailing - are known in the literature as Lazarus movements and they have no doubt given more than one coroner or funeral director quite a turn. They are thought to represent the discharge of spinal cord neurons when, so to speak, they don't know what to do with themselves – because they have been cut off from information from the brain, or higher levels of the cord. But they themselves, and the muscles they connect to, are still alive and capable of some function. And this functional reserve – coupled with the automaticity of stepping and placing – is why Freddie Gray could be seen to attempt, unsuccessfully, to place a leg forward and try to bear weight on it, even as he was being dragged to the van on legs which were rapidly evolving paralysis from his already broken neck. It is why, in a single frame of video, he briefly appears to be standing after being hoisted into a standing position in the back of the van, though at no time is he seen to be completely free from support. He was never able to either walk or stand independently after his neck was broken during the arrest process and before he was put into the van. He didn't get into the van by himself: he couldn't. It wasn't passive, uncooperative resistance – it was real dysfunction. **Gray's spinal cord damage wasn't complete– a point acknowledged by Forensic Pathologist Allan,** and even ultimately by Expert Witness Matthew Ammerman: it was compressed, bruised, and seriously injured, but he still, briefly, retained some function. **It was whole, not severed. And some of his cord was still intact enough to work, as Dr. Allan said in her sworn witness testimony (but not in her autopsy report).** His spinal cord was not "severed", a term persistently used in media reporting and, indeed, by "Expert Witness" neurosurgeon Matthew Ammerman in trial testimony, until he was forced to admit otherwise by a prosecuting attorney. In fact Gray's spinal cord had not been cut: it had suffered a compression injury severe enough to result in ultimately fatal neurological dysfunction, but consistent with some retained function initially. And, again according to Allan's sworn testimony, it was not "crushed" nor severed.

Prior to any trial, Baltimore neurosurgeon Ali Bydon was quoted in the Baltimore Sun as saying that the video of Gray briefly standing in the van did not prove that his neck and spinal cord were uninjured. Noting, as the Medical Director of St. Agnes hospital had done with regard to the preceding victim Jeffrey Alston years ago, that not all function has to disappear at once, Bydon said: "It can be a progressive, cumulative loss of function if the spinal cord is unstable and unprotected".

There are two essential points here. One is that the spinal cord is a complex organ with built-in capacities which are not entirely dependent on information from the brain or other levels above any point of injury. It can be wounded, even fatally, and still briefly retain some function. As it did. The other point is that Gray's spinal cord was neither severed nor crushed: it was severely, and probably irrecoverably, bruised. But it was found at autopsy to be intact.

Did any injury take place in the van? The first rule in the management of even suspected spinal injury is to protect the cord from further damage by immobilization, not by putting the victim in a situation where he may be tossed about and further damage done. Gray was shoved in and out of the van at multiple stops, and also probably dragged upright to some extent at stop 4 and hauled out again at stop 6 when "resuscitation" was attempted. Whatever the extent of the original injury was it was clearly severe, resulting in difficulty breathing and an inability to walk. The extent to which it was worsened in his van trip is unknowable but it is probable that it would have been, as unstable fragments of the spine and discs may have been further shoved against an already damaged spinal cord. The extent to which he might have been rescued, or whether that would ever have been possible had he received prompt medical attention, is also unknowable, but it was the opinion of Expert Witness Soriano that that was possible.

Even with perfect immobilization, *spinal cord injury which will ultimately result in complete paralysis, would not have to be immediately and fully manifest.* Further cell death occurs over an extended period. That the neurosurgical expert witness for the defense, Matthew Ammerman, assumed and testified otherwise reflects either his ignorance on this subject or the mind- altering powers of the $15,000. which he was paid to testify. Among other things, Ammerman was basing his opinion on the appearance of the spinal cord some 8 days after the initial insult and the subsequently evolving deterioration which would have occurred. Ammerman also made much of the fact that, for some minutes after arrest Gray was able to keep breathing, and even to speak, when at autopsy his spinal cord damage was found to be at a level which controlled movement of the diaphragm, the principal muscle in breathing. (Contrary again to media reports, his voice-box was not "crushed"). Gray indeed had immediate difficulty in breathing, asking for his inhaler ("pump"), and to be taken to the hospital for that reason. It was natural for him to relate that to his only previous experience of shortness of breath, namely, his asthma. But asthma wasn't the problem. Jeffrey Alston, a previous victim of a police-broken neck, had also complained of difficulty breathing. In both cases it was interpreted as "asthma", but it is entirely plausible that in both cases the difficulty breathing was related to evolving diaphragmatic paralysis. Not only may the eventual damage be incomplete at that point, but *persons with even complete diaphragmatic paralysis can both breathe and speak: breathing is also supported by thoracic and other cervical musculature.* Use of these so-called "accessory muscles of respiration" comes into play in a variety of situations: exhausted runners may be seen to lean forward, bracing their forearms on, say, a car, as they utilize them. Persons with diaphragmatic paralysis cannot breathe as well or deeply as an uninjured person – they do not have careers as opera singers – but persons with diaphragmatic paralysis from a variety of causes may present to a physician with a (spoken) complaint of shortness of breath. Sooner or later, if the cause of diaphragmatic paralysis is spinal cord injury and the spinal cord level is appropriate, thoracic musculature will fail as well, or the support it offers may be insufficient when challenged. That is why pneumonia is a common threat in immobilized patients. Dondi Johnson, a previous victim, died from pneumonia two weeks after his initial insult. Freddie Gray died because the inflicted injury and subsequent hypoxia – ultimately anoxia, occurring before he arrived at a hospital, and with respiratory impairment also compounded by loss of blood flow in the left vertebral artery- had inflicted enough organ damage to cause ultimate failure.

Finally, there is more than one way to break a neck. See for yourself, Gentle Reader. Get a reasonably long, reasonably dry stick and put it on the ground. Put your foot on it. Then take both ends, or even one end, and bend it up abruptly while you still have your weight on it. It will break. Necks can be broken that way too. It is not necessary to land on your head from an upright position. Necks can be snapped by a Hangman. And necks can be broken by having someone kneel on it as you lie face down on a rigid surface, hands tied behind your back, and you naturally try to raise your head, thereby extending your neck, and someone else grabs both of your legs and abruptly yanks them up towards the back of your neck, folding you up, in the words of the eye-witness who shot the video, "like a piece of origami." That is what the arresting officers did, and that is how his neck was broken. No doubt they didn't mean to, but they did.

It didn't happen in the van.

CHAPTER 8:

What They Said at the Trial

It is not too much to say that the outcome of the Trials of the six charged officers, in the hands of a Judge after the first trial of Porter resulted in a hung jury, was determined before the first person took the stand. To a major extent, the Prosecution had to depend upon proving charges which depended on circumstantial evidence and upon knowing the state of mind of the defendant. Mosby, who brought those charges, certainly should have known better. *Unfortunately, Mosby relied upon the autopsy report and in interpreting it confused autopsy evidence, in the usual sense, with opinion, which the pathologist had derived from what the police told her about the state of the victim and the timing of the injury.* She therefore brought charges which, in greatest part, had to do with an event presumed to take place inside the van. And the media followed suit. This error of construction was the determining factor in the acquittal of the four officers tried – Porter, Nero, Goodson and Rice- and of charges being dropped against the others. It was a calamitous error.

Mosby's choice of the Lead Prosecutor, Michael Schatzow, was also questionable. Of the two principal prosecutors, Michael Schatzow and Janice Bledsoe, Bledsoe had by far the more experience in trials of this nature: she had often been a defender designated to act in the Court-appointed defense of a charged person who was otherwise without representation and, in fact, had represented

Freddie Gray in the past. Lead Attorney Schatzow, however, though considerably older (and male), was relatively inexperienced in trials of this kind: he had previously functioned principally as an attorney for Corporations before retiring from his law firm and becoming Chief Deputy State's Attorney. He had worked on espionage and organized crime cases for the Federal Government, but Saturday-Night- Knife-and-Gun-Club trials were not his thing, let alone the prosecution of criminal trials dependent on medical evidence. In any case, The State Prosecutors had been stuck with having to proceed in an effort to prove the unprovable: their hands were tied as securely as Freddie Gray's had been. They could not approach what should have been an easily winnable homicide case against the arresting officers. That would have been substantiated by a video of the arrest, numerous eyewitnesses, and numerous experts. However, this was not a part of the charges brought. And neither of them informed themselves sufficiently about the medical aspects of the case to challenge the Defense at various key points. Or to argue with Mosby about it, before she announced the charges, relying on "medical evidence" that wasn't. The choice of her expert witnesses was also largely regrettable. In this way, the Judge was also misled. At times the trial action was almost farcical, with the Defense establishing the facts that would have facilitated prosecution of the arresting officers had they been appropriately charged with homicide, and the Prosecution confirming Defense arguments, when they weren't failing to establish certain obvious points.

The most important point to be established in the charges brought, after the determination to bring charges at all, was the timing of Gray's injury. From the point of view of the Police, it was intensely desirable to implant the thesis that the injury happened in the van, not during the arrest. In this they were enormously fortunate. The timing of the injury accepted by Mosby was entirely taken from the opinion of the Forensic Pathologist, Carol Allan. But this constituted an *opinion*, not medical evidence. Unfortunately, because this opinion was embedded in Allan's autopsy report, it became construed as medical evidence. But it wasn't: it was a hand-off from the Police. And they worked hard to try to establish Gray's physical normality until some later point in the van ride, thereby clearing the arresting officers and requiring proof that the others had injured Gray, negligently or deliberately, by the failure to secure him during a deliberately rough ride and failure to get him medical help in a timely fashion.

It helps, at this point, to be clear about the chronology of that ride, which took place in less than an hour and with 5 stops prior to arrival at the destination, Central Booking.

FIRST STOP: at Presbury and Mount streets. TIMING OF ACTION, AS RECORDED: 8:40 A. TO 8:46 AM. THE VAN WAS CALLED AT 8:42. *Video evidence begins at this stop. Gray is seen prone on the cement, hands cuffed behind his back, Officer Miller kneeling on his neck and Officer Nero abruptly forcing both legs up towards the back of his head. Gray can be heard on the video screaming in pain. A Bystander said Gray shouted "Get off my neck, you hurting my neck!" Police confirmed that he said "I can't breathe!" and that he asked for an inhaler. Two officers hoist him up and drag him to the van, assisted by Officer Rice. His legs are functionally useless. At the audible command "Walk!" he makes a primitive attempt at stepping with his left leg, but cannot sustain weight- bearing. A woman is heard shouting: "You broke his fucking legs!" Officers Miller and Nero, assisted by Officer Rice, drag Gray into the van and leave him on his belly, face down, according to multiple witnesses. Nero says he pulled him out again briefly to frisk him, then put him back in the van on the bench. He testifies that Gray stood up and helped get himself onto the bench. A single frame shows Gray against the back and side of the van: at no point can he be said to be free of support, either from the van frame or from officers. There is no evidence that he was ever placed on the bench, and two minutes later he is dragged out feet first from a prone position in the van. Bystanders and a cell phone video show him being shoved in, on his belly.*

SECOND STOP: MOUNT AND BAKER STREET, about two minutes later: 8:52 to 8:54. *The van is briefly halted, allegedly because Gray is causing it to shake. In trial testimony, the Forensic Pathologist Allan would testify that it was possible that the shaking was caused by Gray having a seizure. He is dragged out by Officer*

Nero, and a camera records him "kneeling" while leaning against the back of the van while police shackle his legs. His position, although described as "kneeling", is the position in which he would have landed when dragged out feet first and propped against the van. Nero claims that he then left Gray on the bench at stop 2, but Porter testifies that Gray had again been left face down on his belly, one officer in the van dragging his upper body in while the other shoves his torso and legs in. Testimony differs on whether or not the van was rocking at this stop: the judge points out that it is not seen to be rocking on the available film clip.

THIRD STOP: N. FREMONT AND MOSHER: 8:54 to 8:56. No video is available. *Allegedly it is to check on the prisoner. Goodson briefly looks into the back of the van and calls for someone to check Freddie out.*

FOURTH STOP: DRUID HILL AND DOLPHIN STREETS. 8:59. *Gray asks for "help". Porter tells him to get up, and Gray says he can't. Porter drags him to the bench, variably testifying that he left him on the floor against the bench (testimony to Detective Teel, Task Force Investigative Team) or on the bench with the assistance of Gray (trial testimony). Per Porter's testimony he asks Gray if he wants to go to the hospital, which Gray affirms. Goodson, the van driver, sees him and says that he, Gray, is not going to make it past Central Booking without medical clearance. Porter agrees. However:*

FIFTH STOP: 1600 N. AVE. 9:06. *Under the direction of Officer Rice, the Senior officer who had called for Gray's arrest and was in charge, the van does not go to a hospital but diverts to pick up another passenger, Donta Allen. Officer White arrives and Porter tells her that Gray won't make it through Central Booking. White enters the van. Gray is unresponsive to calling his name and minimally responsive otherwise. White described him as "lethargic". In his initial statement to the police Allen states that he heard loud banging from inside the van, which he interpreted as Gray banging his head against something. Once he got the drugs out of his system, however, Allen rejected the word "loud", and indicated that he couldn't know what might have been banging. In any case, he said, it lasted about 4 seconds.*

SIXTH STOP: 9:24. *Gray is unresponsive, not breathing and without a pulse – in other words, what used to be known as dead. He was leaning against the bench where Porter had placed him and in essentially the same posture, arm and head on the bench, body on the floor. He is partially hauled out head and torso first, and MEDICAL AS-SISTANCE CALLED FOR. He is "resuscitated", first by the untrained Officer Novak who does sternal rubs but not CPR, and then by an arriving medic. GRAY IS TRANSPORTED TO SHOCK TRAUMA AT 9:54. Eight days later he is pro-nounced dead, never having regained consciousness.*

––––

The first officer to be tried was Officer Porter. Porter was initially tried by a jury, which failed to reach an agreement on any of the charges against him. Porter, who had not been actively present at the arrest or at the van until stop 4, was charged with involuntary manslaughter, assault in the second degree, reckless endangerment, and misconduct in office. The jury, composed of 4 white and 8 black jurors, was hung on all counts. We do not know if the votes in general broke down along lines of race or gender, but there was clearly crossover in all votes. Although that trial was ultimately dismissed, there is still instructive testimony given in it that is worth reviewing because it is applicable to the other cases and trials.

Given the nature of the charges the State had to establish , first, that the timing of Gray's injury was settled as occurring at some point during the 45 to 50 mi-nute van ride; second, that the injury was due to a culpable failure to seat-belt Gray, so that, third, he was injured during a deliberately rough ride; fourth, that Gray's requests for medical help were ignored, and finally,, that timely as-sistance might have saved his life. During Porter's jury trial the pertinent Ex-pert Witnesses – Neurosurgeons Mark Soriano for the Prosecution, Matthew Ammerman and Joel Winer for the Defense – and the Forensic Pathologists Dr. Vincent DiMaio and Dr. Joseph Arden – were called upon to establish the timing and consequences of Gray's injury. Dr. Carol Allan, the Forensic Pathologist on the case, was also accepted as an Expert Witness. As the timing of the event had been taken from her report, she was anticipated to be an anchor of the timing. Unfortunately, the claim for medical evidence to support the timing was destroyed by defense lawyer Joseph Murtha: nonetheless this and subsequent trials went forward as though it had been the case the medical evidence established that the injury had occurred during the van ride.

Here is how Defense Attorney Murtha, with a probably inadvertent assist from Prosecutor Bledsoe, established that the Autopsy report statements about the timing of Gray's injury did not constitute medical evidence:

From the Trial Testimony, Dec. 15, 2015:

Bledsoe to Forensic Pathologist Allan, regarding her interpretation of the timing of Gray's injury as occurring sometime after the second van stop:

"What do you base your opinions on?"

Allan: "The autopsy itself and the circumstances, the information gathered from the circumstances surrounding the death as well as the autopsy findings. Substantial presence by the Baltimore City Police and, as we discussed the particulars of a particular death, they offer information. I had a lot of information from the investigating agency...I met with the Police 5 times."

Defense Attorney Murtha: "Who are you relying on to gather that information?"

Allan: "The Police."

Pursuing the issue of injury in the van which, if Gray had been uninjured when he was shoved into the van on his belly, would (according to Allan) have required him to get up while in the van, and to then have a fall or some other direct trauma, Murtha asks:

"You had no physical evidence, no documentary evidence, that shows he actually got up, correct?"

Allan: "Yes."

The subsequent testimony might have been used to establish that Gray was immobilized- by implication, paralyzed – at least from stop 2 on, unravelling the thesis of injury post stop 2:

Murtha: " So stop 2, he's on his stomach, stop 3 no information is available, stop 4 he's head first on his stomach, correct?"

Allan: " It seems like it's the same position all along…"

Murtha: " Is it conceivable that he was in the same position because he couldn't move?"

Allan: "That is speculation I don't agree with…because…the injury that he sustained can only happen…in certain ways…."

In other words, the timing of the injury had not been determined by autopsy findings or other medical evidence, but was *opinion*, derived from Police accounts. Indeed the Autopsy reported presented the timing in a section labelled OPINION. And the injury might have been present BY the second stop – which is to say, from the first stop, on – that is, *at the time of the arrest*. The Defense had no need to go further with that, however, since leaving it where it was might help to clear their clients from the charge of causing the primary injury at a later time by the combination of failure to prevent a fall by seatbelting, and a rough van ride. That was all that was wanted. There was an additional reason for the Defense not to take it further. If, for it to happen in the van, Gray would have had to get up to fall and then fall again, thereby breaking his own neck, and it couldn't be established that he did get up, then *it had to happen before he entered the van*. And the police would have been mad at their defense lawyers for that, as it would have removed the cause of injury from being an accident in the van, leaving it attributable to the arrest process – not an accidental occurrence and at most perhaps a civil offense, but rather, a criminal act. On the other hand, it would have been a gem for the Prosecution to use if they had understood its implications, and if injury by officers before loading Gray into the van had been the charge, which it should have been, but wasn't. As it was, the several trials proceeded under the assumption that the injury happened in the van, and that establishing that timing of that injury was of critical importance in the prosecution and the defense of the involved officers. Allan continued to defend the timing as having occurred sometime after stop 2 and by stop 4.

———

With regard to the second critical point, namely, establishing that the failure to seat-belt Gray was a key determinant – and a foreseeable one, of his injury - The Prosecution did the Defense a great favor by agreeing that the police procedural violation - failure to follow the new directive with regard to seat-belting - which formed the basis of the most serious charges, was not really criminal after all. In the first place, the Defense began by arguing that nobody ever bothered to seat-belt van prisoners. This does not seem like a great argument. Rather lamely, especially in the case of Gray, it was also maintained that to do so would bring the officer and the prisoner so close together that the prisoner might overcome the officer, and/or grab his gun, so it became an issue of officer judgment as to whether or not it was safe to approach so closely. It would appear that it was always a danger, in police opinion. The Defense also argued that *Foreseeable Harm* - in this case, a broken neck arising from a failure to seat-belt Gray- was neither an intentional nor a foreseeable outcome of the failure to seatbelt him in any case. This point rebutted not only charges against Porter, but the charge against all of the officers charged with Assault in the second Degree, which is to say, all of the officers. The arguments here were most succinctly articulated in the trial of Officer Rice who was the ranking Officer involved in Gray's arrest and transport.

Judge Williams, to Prosecutor Schatzow:

"You have alleged…that it was the failure of the Defendant (here, Brian Rice) to seat-belt Mr. Gray in a van…You're not saying that failing to seatbelt in and of itself is a crime, correct?"

Schatzow: "It's a basis for a crime, your Honor, but it's not by itself."

Judge Williams: …"I'm saying failure to seatbelt alone is not a crime, you would agree with that?"

Schatzow: "Yes your Honor."

Now Schatzow could, and should, have gone on to argue that not to seat belt someone was a foreseeable risk for harm, – otherwise, what was the purpose of a seatbelt law? In fact Maryland had had a seatbelt law in place since 2010. It was a primary law – that is, one for which the police could pull you over, without other provocation, for all drivers and passengers under the age of 16, and a secondary law for those over the age of 16 and in a back seat. The self-evident purpose of this law was to reduce the injury rate to passengers and drivers of a motor vehicle. And, just as under Maryland law it is a homicide to fire a gun at someone who is killed by it, even if not deliberately, since the act of firing a gun is to injure or destroy, so the act of *not* seat-belting someone is a foreseeably injurious act. A failure to seat-belt someone would constitute at the very least negligent homicide, if the person died as a consequence of a motor vehicle accident or some other attributable cause. Not being sufficiently re-strained would enable a passenger, for example, the ability to stand up and fall down again and break his own neck, which suggestion was coming down the pike. But Schatzow left the seatbelt issue where it was, which was unfortunate for the prosecution. It was an issue which affected not only Porter but all the other officers charged with assault in the second degree for the same reason. And all of the officers had been charged with second-degree assault, which was a foreseeable harm, if the vehicle were in motion. Thus, writing in the Rice case decision, Judge Williams said: *"In order for the defendant's failure to seatbelt Mr. Gray to rise to the level of reckless conduct and create a risk of death or serious physical injury, there has to be some use and movement of the vehicle…the simple placement of a person in a vehicle that is not used, without seat-belting him, cannot and does not constitute a crime. Again, the State has failed to show that the defendant was aware…that his conduct created a risk of death or serious physical injury."* In his opinion concerning the Goodson trial, Judge Williams wrote: *"The court finds that the State has failed to meet its burden that the defendant was aware, or should have been aware, that failing to seat belt Mr. Gray created a high risk to, and disregard for human life."* While of course in the specifics of the injury under discussion – a broken neck - that was true, Schatzow never argued—as he should have done—that the purpose of seatbelts is to prevent ANY injury while riding in a vehicle. Since Gray was obviously going to be in a moving vehicle, he was foreseeably put at risk – endangered – by not being belted. Perhaps Schatzow thought the point was too obvious to need articulation, but it resulted in the judge turning his decision upon the narrow point of whether or not movement of the van, by another driver, had been initiated and thus injury was foreseeable. The opinion, based on the nearly spurious distinction between the act of failing to seat-belt a passenger and foreseeing that the vehicle of placement would subsequently be in motion, would of course have been the same in a Porter trial if it had come to judgment.

Because the issue of foreseeable harm arising from an unbuckled seatbelt was never pursued, the narrow interpretation of that failure to seat-belt as a stand-alone act prevailed. To the extent that any charge was dependent on it, it was not a crime. So, no crime, then no guilt, no punishment. There went that one. In thus reasoning so narrowly, Judge Williams was clearly open to criticism. All that was wanted was the actors chasing each other around and hitting themselves on their own behinds with big paddles. It might have been funny, if the outcome hadn't been so sad, the outcome of the entirety of the trials so unjust.

———

The point about Porter (and by implication others) failing to obtain timely medical help was neither disputed nor pursued, although it was potentially damning. It might have been brought against several officers – Porter (who had asked Gray at both the fourth and fifth stops whether he wanted medical help, only to ignore the affirmative answers), or the arresting officers, when Gray was acknowledged to have said "I can't breathe" before even being loaded in the van. The charges would have been applicable to Rice, Goodson and White as well, as they were aware of Gray's pleas and Goodson saw (by stop 3, when he called for someone to come help check Gray out) and said (by stop 4) that he might not make it to Central Booking without a hospital trip first. Porter said the same thing to Officer White at stop 5.

Porter, April 17 2015, to Detective Teel of the Force Investigative Team, re stop 4:

"And I say {to Gray} What's up? What's going on with you?" And he doesn't say anything and he's like, 'help me, help me up': I pull him up. And I say, 'What's the deal? You need a medic?' I offer. He doesn't ask for the hospital. I offered it to him. 'You need to go to the hospital or something?" And he says, he says, "Yes."'

Detective Teel: *"And when you helped him up, did you help him onto the bench or did you just help him sit up, already like, still on the floor?"*

Porter: *"He was still on the floor."*

Teel: *"Okay…you and, uh, wagon Officer Caesar {Goodson} agreed that he should go to Bon Secours, I mean the hospital –"*

Officer Porter: *"Correct"*.

Was it Departmental Policy to ask, or did something about Gray suggest that he might have needed to go to the hospital? Obviously, the latter. And also of note is the fact that Porter would, in subsequent sworn testimony, reverse his statement about where he had left Gray, subsequently saying it was on the bench. That was an important deception. It implied (as Porter went on to say) that Gray had helped Porter put him on the bench at that stop, so he must have had the muscle strength to do so at that time. A normal physical status would, incorrectly, have been inferred from this: thus, the argument went, he was still uninjured at the time of stop 4. Porter claimed that he would have been unable to lift Gray onto the bench alone, as lifting Gray's dead weight would have been impossible. But any fireman would tell you otherwise: they do the equivalent of that all the time. And Gray, at 140 lbs., was a comparative lightweight. The prosecution forgot to make that point.

Apparently also forgotten were Gray's repeated statements that he couldn't breathe. Witnesses to the arrest reported that he had said that before he was ever put in the van. So did the earlier victim Jeffrey Alston, because he, like Gray, had a rapidly evolving paralysis of the diaphragm impeding his breathing. But that issue, inexplicably, inexcusably, was never raised. It might have implicated the arresting officers, which wasn't wanted.

Porter's first, jury, trial, having ended in a mistrial, Porter was to be tried again. A second trial, this time a bench trial before Judge Williams, was scheduled and initiated but never completed.

Associated with the issue of failure to obtain help in a timely fashion was, of course, the question of whether or not timely assistance might have saved Gray's life. But first, the TIME of "timely" had to be established. Expert Witnesses – most notably, Neurosurgeons Mark Soriano, Matthew Ammerman and Joel Winer and the Forensic Pathologists Vincent DiMaio and Joseph Arden were called upon to establish the timing and consequences of Gray's injury. Dr. Carol Allan, the Forensic Pathologist on the case, was also accepted as an Expert Witness for the State. As the overall framework had been taken from her report, she was anticipated to be an anchor of the timing. Unfortunately for the Prosecution the claim for medical evidence to support that framework – inside the van- had early on been destroyed by Defense Attorney Murtha. Nonetheless all the trials went forward as though this had not been the case. The charge of Reckless Endangerment stemmed not only from Porter's failure to seatbelt Gray, in accordance with the recent Departmental directive, but from his failure to immediately call for medical help when Gray affirmed to him that he wanted to go to the hospital. He affirmed this to Goodson repeatedly, at both stops 4 and 5. And, earlier, why did Goodson, after glancing at Gray at stop 3, call for assistance for someone to help "check out" the prisoner, and why, at stop 4, did he tell Porter – who agreed – that Gray would never make it through Central Booking without a medical stop first? The point about failing to secure medical help for Gray when he asked for it was never contested, though it was potentially damning. Ultimately in any case the judge would have dismissed it, accepting the statements from the Defendants that no one had any visible reason to think Gray was in need of medical attention, and saying that the police simply couldn't be expected to take everyone who said they wanted to go to the hospital, to the hospital.

Judge Williams: *The State argues that it was obvious that Mr. Gray was in need of medical care. This was based on Porter's interactions with Mr. Gray at Stop 4 and 5 where, after Porter asked Gray if he, 'Wanted to go to the hospital', Gray said 'Yes'… .If this were the standard, then every time one officer told another that a transportee wanted to go to the hospital and was not transported, the person who failed to transport could be charged with a crime."*

Not a bad idea, actually. However, it might have been queried– then why did Porter ask the question? Repeatedly, at both stops 4 and 5? Why did Goodson, earlier, at stop 3, glance at Gray and proceed to call for assistance in checking him out? Why at stop 4 did Goodson say to Porter – who agreed – that Gray would never make it past Central Booking and should be transported to hospital?

———

Obtaining any information from Porter in his trial before Judge Williams was initially disputed on procedural grounds. Pre-trial, in the "investigation" conducted by the Police, he had been immunized: that, in effect, was equivalent to taking the Fifth. Anything he said based on the pre-trial testimony could not be used against him. It prevented any further testimony on the subjects on which he had already been questioned from being used against him; hence, the defense argued, there was no point in asking him to testify again. But, Prosecution argued, the contrast between what he said initially, to the Force Investigation Taskforce (FIT) composed of Police, and what he said at the trial, might have been relevant in another Officer's trial. The most important issue had to do with the position in which Gray had been left by Porter at stop 5. Initially Porter had not made any mention of Gray helping him when he allegedly placed him on the van bench from a prone position. And, in fact, in the FIT investigation he said that he had left him on the floor of the van, leaning against the bench but not on it. The point becomes critical because Porter said Gray had helped him when he, Porter, put him on the bench. If Gray did help get himself up, several "Expert Witnesses" would say that he had enough muscle power at that stop to dispute the claim of prior injury. The Prosecution understood that anything said at a later trial could not be used against him, but they were not trying to implicate Porter directly. They wanted to establish contradictions in two versions of his testimony in order to establish that his credibility was suspect. Porter had also denied being close enough to the van to see which officers were involved with Gray at stop 2, but video film showed that he had been, another challenge to his credibility. Challenged about the discrepancy between there being no mention of Gray helping Porter place him on the bench at stop 4, and his trial testimony that Gray had helped move himself, Porter (who was ultimately permitted to testify as a witness in subsequent trials) said that he hadn't realized it was an important point at the FIT investigation. Now he did. But in his testimony to the Force Investigative Team, Porter told Detective Teel that he had left Gray on the floor. Previously that statement had been used to help place the timing of the injury to some later point in the van ride. But that was a weak challenge, one concerning a plausible omission of statement rather than a conflicting statement. The *conflicting* statements went unchallenged. Porter in all probability had altered them to protect his fellow officers.

Although Porter was ultimately allowed to testify, to a limited extent, in the other trials, a decision after his own bench trial testimony with regard to his own guilt was not reached as the charges against him were dropped before the trial was completed.

The second trial held was that of Officer Nero. Nero was one of the arresting officers who captured Gray, although Miller in testimony said that he, Miller, had made the arrest alone, and "without incident or undue force". He described Gray placing himself on the ground. A subsequent version described Gray as "combative", and it was claimed that an illegal knife was found on him when Miller, now assisted by Nero, took him "into custody." Be that as may be, the first we see of the three of them on video shows Gray prone on the sidewalk, hands cuffed behind his back, Miller (who had estimated his own weight as 240 lbs, thereby outweighing Gray by 100 lbs) kneeling on his neck while Nero grabs both legs together and twists them upwards towards Gray's skull while Gray screams in pain. Nero was thus one of the two arresting officers who were direct participants in the process and event which broke Gray's neck. Gray was never shown to walk independently thereafter. But instead of being charged with this eminently provable forceful act which led to Gray's death, Nero was charged with assault in the second degree intentional, assault in the second degree negligent, - again, the seatbelt issue – and with misconduct in office and false imprisonment. False imprisonment was a charge that never should have been brought: it was easily defeated by reference to laws passed in 1968 (Ohio v. Terry) and in 2000 (Illinois v. Wardlow) which made it permissible to detain a person – any "suspicious" person – seen leaving a high crime area. These laws had been endorsed by the Supreme Court. In any case Gray never made it to prison: he died first. Mosby and the Prosecution team should have been aware of this. Bledsoe apparently was not: she no doubt was reacting to the sheer unreasonableness at arresting someone walking with friends and coming away from a place to get coffee (it was closed) on an early Sunday morning when there was no indication of a crime having been committed.

Bledsoe: *"We believe that the search and arrest without justification are assault, your honor…there's no question about that."* The judge, however, was incredulous.

Judge Williams, in the closing arguments phase of the Nero case: *"So every time there's an arrest without probable justification – is it a crime? I'm trying to make sure it was a criminal assault. Touching Freddie Gray is assault?"* In his opinion he wrote: *"The State concedes that pursuant to Wardlow and Terry {there was a right to stop Freddie Gray}"*.

Bledsoe might have responded that touching Gray in such a way as to break his neck was, but she was not, unfortunately, empowered to make that argument. It wasn't part of the charges.

Assault in the second degree negligent was a reasonable charge – the failure to seat-belt issue – but "assault intentional" was not, since it is obviously impossible to prove a state of mind absent other, more direct, evidence.

Misconduct in office was a trivial, civil offense under the law (whatever it may sound like), to which Nero pled guilty and was rewarded with "minor disciplinary action" - 5 days of suspension, without pay.

Nero was found not guilty on all charges and subsequently brought suit against Mosby.

The third trial was that of the van driver, Officer Goodson. The charges against him were the most serious. He was charged with second-degree depraved heart murder, involuntary manslaughter, second-degree assault, manslaughter by vehicle by means of gross negligence, manslaughter by vehicle by means of criminal negligence, misconduct in office by failure to secure prisoner, and failure to render aid. The murder and manslaughter charges depended upon establishing that, first, Gray had been injured as a consequence of a rough van ride; second, that that such a van ride was deliberate, and third, that Goodson was aware of the probability, or high probability, of injury occurring as a result of that ride. It was the seat-belt issue again, already determined in the mind of the judge.

The charges of gross and criminal negligence required proof of a state of mind, which was of course not possible. (Goodson's testimony might have been of value concerning the conduct of other officers at stops 1 and 2, but he was not allowed to testify directly to those points because of complex issues involving prior statements). What was the nature of the so-called "rough ride" van trip that needed to be proved?

It was in fact what had been described by Dondi Johnson in 2005, who told his physicians that he had been handcuffed and subjected to a deliberately rough ride. Subsequent persons subjected to this treatment had described it also. And whatever then Police Commissioner Batts told his officers about the usual excuse having to do with avoiding a dog as the necessity for an abrupt, jerky ride when charged - "You better come with the dog – " the practice had persisted. Two weeks after Gray's death a photograph of a sign inside a van saying *We hope you enjoyed your van ride. Cuz we shure did*, surfaced. The Commissioner pitched a fit. A spokesperson for the Department said it was absolutely unacceptable, and then the sign disappeared again. But not necessarily the practice.

A rough ride was virtually necessary to substantiate the claimed timing of injury to the van ride, and certainly necessary to establish guilt on the part of the van driver. Goodson, the first officer to call for assistance for Gray, became a fall guy. Both the Pathologist, Allan, and the Expert Forensic Pathologist Witness, Arden, said that it had to have happened because Gray somehow managed to stand up and then lose his balance as the van jerked around. Di-Maio, Arden and Ammerman said that it had to have happened after stop 5. If the van hadn't been jerked around, they would be back to the seat-belt issue again. But Donta Allen, who had been a passenger in the same van since stop 5, denied that the ride had been rough, and, as there was no video or other corroborating witness to establish the facts one way or the other, the charges against Goodson that were based on that had to be dismissed if that argument of the time injured were to be maintained. As it happened Goodson had no previous charges and no reputation for such activity, but Judge Williams wouldn't have allowed such testimony anyway. The question was the intent of the moment. Judge Williams, in his decision on the Goodson case: *"If there was evidence that the defendant intended to give Mr. Gray a rough ride as alleged; it may have been sufficient to show that the defendant caused his death but, as noted, this Court does not find that the evidence was the intended action of the defendant."*

And, with regard to the issue of failing to obtain medical help after Gray affirmed that he wanted to go to the hospital, other testifying officers, in witness statements, had agreed that Gray showed no outward and visible signs of injury or the need for medical help before the denouement at stop 6, when somebody called a medic. (A call had to be placed twice, and the help arrived in about 20-30 minutes). Goodson was found Not Guilty. Williams wrote that *"This Court has already determined beyond a reasonable doubt that the evidence does not show that the defendant know or should have known that Mr. Gray was in medical distress before stop 6."*

But Goodson had seen this at stop 3, and articulated it to Porter at stop 4. As stated, it was a decision at variance with the strongest evidence. Had this decision been based on the issue of chain of command, Goodson not feeling empowered to take Gray directly without an order to do so, it might have held up better, but even then it might have been successfully challenged. Here is what Michael Lyman, a Professor of Criminal Justice with direct experience in policing and the author of 8 books concerning police responsibilities with custodial prisoners, had to say, when Schatzow asks him about the responsibility of an officer when a prisoner says he can't breathe and can't get up by himself:

Dr. Lyman: *"First of all, make a determination of where the nearest hospital is and be sure that that individual is immediately transported to the hospital...The responsibility...it's made worse by the fact that this same officer has the information from the previous stop at Druid Hill and Dolphin (i.e. stop 4), so the individual was not taken as they should've been to the hospital from the Druid Hill location...It's as simple as that, and I think the demand should have been made of supervisory personnel at that point that this person needs to go to the hospital immediately."*

Schatzow: *"And, does the officer have the option of calling a medic, that is seeking to have medical attention come to the scene as opposed to taking the prisoner to the hospital?*

Dr. Lyman: *"That's absolutely an option."*

———

The fourth trial was that of Officer Rice. Rice was the officer technically in charge of the whole process: his was the senior rank, he ordered the chase and the arrest, and he helped shove Gray into the van. He ordered him pulled out and shackled. He failed to get him medical help despite the complaint of "I can't breathe" and the unchallenged fact that on at least 2 occasions Gray affirmed that he wanted to go to a hospital. Also, Goodson had said that he wasn't going to pass Central Booking and needed instead to go to a hospital. But Rice ordered the van to go pick up another arrestee, Donta Allen, instead. Rice was charged with involuntary manslaughter, misconduct in office, assault in the second degree and false arrest. The last 2 charges were already headed for dismissal on the same grounds that they had been previously dismissed. Assault involves aggressive and intentional physical contact, for which there was no documentation. Involuntary manslaughter revisited the seatbelt issue. Failure to order or perform seat-belting was interpreted as failure to follow a general directive, for which conviction on a criminal charge was not possible: Rice pled guilty to this instance of misconduct in office. All charges against Rice were therefore dismissed on July 16, 2015.

As to the issue of timely assistance being potentially life-saving for Gray, If the testimony of the police officers was misleading – their defending idea of visible injury being visible bleeding, or obviously fractured bones – the testimony of several of the designated expert witnesses was worse. What did the Expert Witnesses say? Of the neurosurgeons, Soriano (a Prosecution witness) was the one who reflected informed neurosurgical opinion – as far as he went. But first the issue of what was "timely" had to be settled. The two issues ran together.

Soriano was up first, after Allan, who simply had said that it was sometime after stop 2, or between stops 2 and 4. But Allan's testimony laid very important groundwork, by testifying that *Gray's cord had been bruised but not transected*, and that, therefore, not all neurological function would have been immediately lost. The finding of partial injury was based on actual autopsy medical evidence, not opinion. And that, in turn, could certainly been taken to imply that at a certain point after the injury – with prompt attention – he might have been salvageable. Not restored to normality, certainly, but alive.

Attorney Bledsoe: *"And, can you tell…was his spinal cord, was it cut in half,…what was the damage in terms o the spinal cord?"*

Dr. Allan: *"No, it was not cut in half or actually cut into…So, it was pinched. Pinched to such an extent that it was functionally cut through, but anatomically, it's not…it's whole."*

From this testimony it might appear that Allan supported the thesis that the loss of function would have been instantaneous but, curiously, she subsequently reversed this opinion. At times her testimony seemed self-contradictory, or confused. Allan went on to allude to the possibility of further damage after the original insult that could have been caused by movement, but also by the natural progression of such an injury. Although she did not specifically offer the analogy, the idea is comparable to the delay in the appearance of bruising and swelling after a blow.

Allan: "*...Because he had fractures on the left side of the neck...it meant...that it was unstable...So that meant that any kind of movement after the primary injury occurred was going to cause more injury. So...*"

But here Allan was cut off by Prosecuting Attorney Bledsoe, who perhaps sensed that this could be an argument for the original injury occurring outside the van and during the arrest. Nonetheless, Allan went on to testify that immediately after the injury, Gray would have been able to breathe and speak. She implied both that further movement of an unstable fracture and the natural course of any injury could result in later, not necessarily immediate, functional loss. Of note, she also made the point that the images obtained once Gray got to the hospital could not be used to infer what his injury had immediately been like.

Bledsoe: "*At that time, given this injury to Mr. Gray, would he have been able to speak right after the injury?*"

Allan: "*Yes, right after the injury...this goes back to what actually the injury was that Mr. Gray had at the time of the incident?...But, was that present at the time of the immediate injury? We're not going to know...So, the scans at 1 hour and the scans at 8 hours showed pretty much a complete injury...usually the injuries are not totally functionally transected...there's 25% of individuals who have a spinal cord injury are going to show deterioration of their neurological function...everything swells...that's exactly what happens in the immediate phase of injury, but it happens in subsequent. {subsequently}.*"

Attorney Bledsoe: "*What is the difference between...complete and incomplete concerning Mr. Gray's injuries?*"

Allan: ..."*It means that, in the injury to the spinal cord is not uniform across the width of the spinal cord...then you can get a partial quadriplegia, meaning that there's going to be neurological deficits in all four limbs, but they can be complete on one side and ...*"

they can be partial on the other side…there could still be muscular control at some point on one side of the body…So, he could speak. He would – so, he would be able to breathe."

Dr. Soriano, a practicing neurosurgeon and experienced Expert Witness, was up next after Allan. Not only had he often been in that role – 50 -75 times, by his own estimate - but this was the second time he had testified about a neck broken by the Baltimore Police Department. Ten years earlier, he had been an Expert Witness in the Dondi Johnson case of 2005. He must have thought they did nothing else.

Dr. Soriano agreed with Dr. Allan concerning the fact that the damage to Gray's spinal cord had been incomplete and that not all neurologic manifestations need be immediately manifest.

Attorney Schatzow: *"And in this particular case, do you have an opinion ….whether the injury suffered by Mr. Gray was complete at the time the injury was suffered or incomplete?"*

Dr. Soriano: *"It was not complete."*

Schatzow: *"And when we talk about some function ——-…can you tell us given the location of the injury…what function he had after the injury?"*

Soriano: *" Well, I would say…he probably may have had some function below the neck for his arms and legs, although we don't know exactly how much…He was probably still able to breathe and speak on his own, at least temporarily, and then, obviously, it progressed to the point where he couldn't talk, couldn't breathe, and then he lost oxygen supply to the brain."*

Schazow: *"Do you have an opinion to a reasonable degree of medical certainty whether, once Mr. Gray, suffered the injury that you describe, he would have benefited from prompt medical attention?"*

Soriano: *"Yes."* And the opinion that he had was also affirmative.

Dr. Matthew Ammerman, also a neurosurgeon, did not agree with Dr. Soriano about the timing of the injury in relation to acknowledged signs and symptoms. Or with the autopsy report. Or, on several points, with authoritative literature or the established experience of clinicians in the field. Moreover, although he, like Soriano, said that he had reviewed the autopsy report, pertinent radiological studies, and Gray's medical record, what he said was not consistent with those sources.

Attorney Murtha: *"Based on your review of the materials, education, training, experience, do you have an opinion …whether the injury suffered by Mt. Gray was complete at the time of the injury?"*

Dr. Ammerman: *"I believe he had a complete spinal cord injury at the time of the injury…that would imply complete respiratory failure …with a complete los of function below the C4-C5 level…He could not say he was short of breath, because he would not be able to speak…when your spinal cord is damaged, you lose immediate function within milliseconds…when someone has a spinal cord like this, they develop…as I said, a flaccid paralysis. They can't offer any assistance in being moved…it's like moving dead weight."*

Attorney Murtha: *"Do you have an opinion…that his condition would have been altered with immediate medical attention?"*

Dr. Ammerman: *"I do not believe."*

Attorney Murtha: *"…Do you have an opinion…whether Mr. Gray suffered this injury between stops #2 and #4?"*

Dr. Ammerman: *"I do not think this type of injury could have occurred {then}."*

Since Ammerman felt that that Gray's injury would have rendered him instantly paralyzed and unable to breathe or speak, and since Gray was speaking

– a bit – at stop 4, Ammerman maintained that the injury must have occurred between stops 5 and 6 (logically, of course, it would be between stops 4 and 6). But Ammerman was also maintaining that Gray's cord had been "transected", or completely cut through, when he was injured. In the Rice trial, he was forced to admit that this was not the case.

Attorney Schatzow: *"So Dr. Ammerman, …do you recognize this as a picture of Mr. Gray's spinal cord at autopsy?"*

Dr. Ammerman: *"That is correct…"*

Schatzow: *"Okay, and the spinal cord is not transected, is it?"*

Ammerman: *"From the point of view of being cut?"*

Schatzow: *"Isn't that what transection means, to be severed?"*

Ammerman: *"Yes, that would be the interpretation of the word."*

Schatzow: *"Right, as opposed to being compressed, correct?"*

Ammerman: *"Yeah, you could use contused, compressed."*

Schatzow: *"And this spinal cord was not cut, correct?"*

Ammerman then tried to substitute something that he certainly knew to be an artifact of the autopsy, nor the injury:

Ammerman: *"I'm not sure, and I can't point to the screen, there does appear to be some type of focal opening of the covering and exposure of the inside elements that would imply it was cut."*

Schatzow: *"Well, it's not just from this image. You've seen other images of the spinal cord, you know that it was not completely severed, don't you?...And to the extent that it is not 100% compromise, then there is still some ability for the spinal cord to function in the area that is not compromised?"*

Ammerman: *"I guess so."*

Ammerman is defeated. He has had to admit that total loss of function would not be immediate.

———

Dr. Vincent DiMaio, a then self-employed Forensic Pathologist, was called as an Expert Witness for the Defense. They must have been sorry, he was really pretty bad. Living in Texas, he began by using the legal definition of Homicide vs. Accident as it is in Texas but not in Maryland, not the forensic definitions as stated by the National Board of Medical Examiners (NAME). On the basis of this irrelevancy he stated that he would have classified Gray's broken neck as an accident. He also disagreed with Dr. Allan's (and Dr. Soriano's) opinion that Gray's injury had occurred by the 4th stop, holding that the injury had occurred from violent force impact in the van and would be immediately manifest as loss of all function. Therefore, the injury had to occur after the fifth stop, when Gray was still apparently alive, and before the 6th stop, when he was really dead. To make this work he had to discount the testimony of the other witnesses, including the Defendant, but never mind.

The Defense gave up as soon as he said that what had happened had been an accident – which was, after all, what they wanted to hear, not an inadequate explanation of why DiMaio thought so – but the Prosecution was more persistent.

Attorney Schatzow: *"In terms of what the defendant said about Mr. Gray at stop #4 being...on his stomach, hands cuffed behind his back, legs shackled saying 'I can't* breathe", *asking for help to get up and then responding in the affirmative that he wanted a medic or to go to the hospital....it's your testimony that that can't possibly have been the result of his having broken his neck before that time?"*

DiMaio: *"Yes sir."*

Schatzow: *"Completely impossible?"*

DiMaio: *"Yes sir."*

Schatzow: *"Okay. Based on the autopsy, do you have an explanation for what injury he suffered that caused him to ask Mr. Porter for help there?"*

DiMaio: *"Maybe, being on the floor, which is kind of narrow. The autopsy itself doesn't show anything but, after all, don't forget the autopsy is done long after the event."*

Schatzow:*" Dr., the spine – let me try to one more time, please. The spinal cord was impacted between C4 and C5, correct?...That's a yes or no, isn't it?"*

DiMaio: *"That's asking are you still beating your wife? Let me explain something, sir."*

Judge Williams: ***"You may not."***

Even the judge seems to have given up. Schatzow however kept trying.

Schatzow: *"You would agree, would you not, that gross negligence is a sufficient basis for a medical examiner to commit homicide?"*

DiMaio: *"No."*

Schatzow: *"No? Didn't you say that in the book you wrote when you talked about decubitus ulcers?"*

DiMaio: *"Okay."*

Scharow went on to establish that Allan's boss, Dr. David Fowler, had signed off on her report designating homicide, and that he was, as DiMaio knew, the Chairman of the Board of NAME. This did not appear to carry any weight with DiMaio, who in disagreeing with Allan's assessment was implicitly disagreeing with Dr Fowler.

Schatzow: *"Prior to your testimony,, have you read any of the testimony in this case?"*

DiMaio: *"No, I mean I just came here for the trial."*

Schatzow: *"I know you just came here for the trial. I'm just asking you whether you had been furnished with the testimony of any of the other experts who testified here?"*

DiMaio:*"Oh, no, oh, no, I mean, RIGHT, YEAH, NO."*

The Prosecution rested.

Defense could not resist one parting shot at this unhelpful Expert.

Attorney Murtha: *" When you were chief medical examiner, were there other medical examiners that may have disagreed with your opinion?"*

DiMaio: *"Sure."*

Murtha: *"Happens all the time?"*

DiMaio: *"It happens all the time."*

―――

Not having fared very well with the presentation of the Defense Forensic Pathologist Dr. DiMaio, Defense thought to try again with a different one and introduced Forensic Pathologist Dr. Jonathan Arden. One has the impression that he was a rather hasty find. He was accepted as an Expert Witness without having his credentials being produced, as there was a stipulation that he would testify in only certain areas. He did not have a stellar past, having previously been fired as Medical Examiner in D.C. for certain inadequacies and irregularities in office. He subsequently set up in private practice, so he was a Forensic Pathologist available for hire. Like Ammerman, he wanted to argue from findings that occurred a week after Gray's injury and he essentially dismissed any functional distinction between a complete and an incomplete cord injury, until Judge Williams forced him to acknowledge that the spinal cord damage even at autopsy was found to be incomplete. He added nothing new except to say, incorrectly, that the bloody foam found on Gray's face at stop 6 had to indicate a traumatic nasal injury. This was not found at autopsy (pulmonary hemorrhage from the struggle to breathe is the probable explanation). Arden also did not appear to be familiar with the forensic definition of homicide, and confused "volitional act" with "intent to injure". Hearing no evidence to confirm the latter, he said he would have classified Gray's death as an accident.

Dr. Arden: *"So, an unforeseen, unexpected, or some in my field would say, unintentional injury leading to death is the very definition for manner of death purposes of accident."*

Schatzow tried to go after the "unforeseen" aspect of the definition by asking Arden if he was familiar with the previous history of unsecured people injured in police van rides, which might have provided a clue to broken necks associated with police van rides without a seatbelt, but the judge would not allow it.

Nobody spent much time in questioning Arden: anything he had to say had already been taken down in examining Ammerman and DiMaio.

So Expert Witnesses disagreed with each other over the course of the trials. Dr. Allan and Dr. Soriano said the injury occurred between stops 2 and 4; Dr, Joel Winer, a neurosurgeon who briefly testified at the Goodson trial, said stops 4-6; Drs. Ammerman and Arden went with between stops 5 and 6. Allan and Soriano said that prompt medical attention after the injury might have helped Gray, or been life-saving: Ammerman said it would not have been. Dr. Allan said it could only have occurred in one way, namely, from Gray somehow managing to extract himself from a 19 inch wide space while on his belly with his arms cuffed behind his back and his legs shackled, and then falling on his head (which at autopsy had no pertinent signs of traumatic impact) in such a way as to break his own neck and land in his original position. That was disputed by another Forensic Pathologist. Allan and Soriano said that some function could persist after his initial injury, which Ammerman was ultimately forced to admit. Who was right about what? The argument about which stop Gray was injured at was irrelevant to begin with, as it had to be, given the misplaced charges based on the assumption that it had happened in the van. It was like disputing the number of angels that could fit on the head of a pin. What can be essentially taken away from these arguments is that there was no hard medical factual evidence to support any timing, only opinion, acknowledged speculation and misinformation. Of note, Ammerman also dismissed the possibility of Gray's alleged kicking in the van as potentially being due to a seizure - at stop 2? (Allan) or at stop 5? (The Police). In any case, Ammerman said that it could not possibly been due to a seizure since, he said, a brain deprived of oxygen could not seize. If he had bothered to look it up, or to ask someone, he might have learned that hypoxic seizures are well recognized. In fact, they are the most common cause of seizures among certain classes of infants, namely, those deprived of oxygen at birth. Any neurologist could have told him that sections of brain abruptly deprived of their blood supply, as in a stroke or brain hemorrhage, may present as seizures or go on to become seizure foci, or both. Had he carefully read the medical admission note, he would have learned that in hospital Gray was given anticonvulsant medications because of recurrent seizures. And, inexcusably, he had initially wanted to argue that the extent of the damage to the cord represented at an autopsy taking place 9 days after the injury – with intervening manipulations, operation, and the natural progression of injury – was representative of the original damage. As for information that is in the literature and widely known (even busy neurosurgeons may be expected to read): it is understood that delayed manifestations of injury happen both on the clinical level, and at the cellular level which underlies that.

From the journal <u>Spine</u>: *It is now generally accepted that SCI (spinal cord injury) is a two-step process involving primary and secondary mechanisms. The primary mechanism involves the initial mechanical injury due to local deformation and energy transformation, whereas the secondary mechanism encompasses a cascade of biochemical and cellular processes and may cause ongoing cellular damage and even cell death.*

Ammerman attempted to mislead about the implications of photographic evidence showing a cord with its opening cut during the autopsy procedure. He also had to be forced into admitting that incomplete injury was compatible with residual function. His testimony was ignorant at best and venal at worst.

———

There is also the issue of what didn't make it to the trial. There was disputation about the information gathered by Detective Dawnyello Taylor at the FIT investigation. She felt it was not adequately represented at the trial, and said so, and she was in some sense removed by the Prosecutors. There were cell phone conversations between the charged Officers, taking place before the charges were placed: subpoenas for them were submitted to the Police, who somehow failed to process them in a timely fashion, so that they were never obtained by the prosecution. And, most devastatingly, witness testimony was virtually suppressed. Only witnesses unavoidably called – Brandon Ross, who had been with Gray at the start of the fatal chase; Donta Allen, who had been in the van with Gray and reversed his earlier statement about what he heard then – really had to be called. But in a post-trials interview with reporters Schatzow said that he had never even heard of some of the others, even though they had been interviewed on tv news stations. There were CD recordings of 23 witness statements which were requested from the Police under the Freedom of Information Act. They were last seen (or heard, or heard of) when they were given to a now-retired FBI agent for delivery to the Department of Justice. No doubt they were delivered. And it would be difficult to believe that copies had not been kept by the Police. If so – they have apparently gone missing.

Given the charges as they were, the Prosecution would not really have wanted to hear them. Witness after witness, as interviewed by the press and on television and as recorded on Youtube, knew that Gray's neck had been broken by the arresting officers. His screams of pain – which can still be heard on recorded cell phone footage-and the undeniable dysfunction of his legs, said by the police to represent "combativeness" and some form of passive resistance, are what they look like: evolving paralysis from a broken neck. Eye-witnesses are not always, or entirely, reliable. Several persons were sure that Gray had been tazed, but that was not born out by reliable investigation. One person said that he saw Gray being beaten, but that was not mentioned by others. They were perhaps interpreting his dysfunction in terms of other incidents familiar to them. But many more witnesses knew what they saw and could interpret it consistently with the others: they knew that it didn't happen in the van. All agreed on the point that he had been injured before the van ride. They saw the Police officers break his neck, and they knew which ones. Here, for example, is what Alethea Booze, would have said, as quoted in the New York Times about his alleged "combative" screaming: "He wasn't hollering until two officers put that knee in his back and he was screaming…Everybody was screaming , 'Call the ambulance, call the ambulance,' and the officers didn't do anything."

And what perhaps is most notable of all: no one person, or persons, were ever actually charged with breaking Gray's neck. Curiously, though, at the end of the trials, his neck was still broken, he was still dead.

CHAPTER 9:

Ethics, The Medical Profession and Freddie Gray

Response from a spine surgeon asked to access list-serves with regard to comments about the timing of Freddie Gray's' Injury:

I agree with your interpretation of the video…one of my friends is a social worker in the Hopkins system. She had mentioned that discussions of the Gray case were going to happen…I know for a fact they have had that very conversation with spine surgeons from Hopkins and the University of Maryland…I do not know the outcome.

Response from another spine surgeon, when asked if he/she would be willing to speak to the NYT with regard to the timing of Gray's injury. The surgeon agreed, from seeing the arrest video, that Gray's neck had been broken before he entered the van.

I'd rather not, but I'd still like to have coffee with you the next time you are in town.

———

The Ethics of medical practice has multiple dimensions. Broadly speaking, medical ethics are grouped around four axes: *Autonomy, Beneficence, Non-ma-*

leficence, and *Justice*. These principles are usually presented in a four-square box, but in reality they are more like a Venn diagram, with its overlapping fields. The history of the evolution of articulated principles of medical ethics has shaped what they are, and are not. All of these principles interact in many cases, but it is the last principal that concerns us in the Freddie Gray case.

Writings on medical ethics have a long history, and date back to centuries BCE. Initially such writings came from a time when the physician and patient had a one-on-one encounter of an intimate, personal nature, and concerned the behavior of the physician towards the patient. That orientation continues to be reflected in the modern ethical principal of **AUTONOMY**, which in the context of medical ethics constitutes a respect for the patient to make medical decisions for him or her self. It therefore is in implicit conflict with a Paternalistic style of decision making and, indeed, information-giving, on which decision making must be based. Patients can't make their own decisions about a mode of treatment or care unless they know what they have, and what the implications of that, and of treatment, are. (Increasingly, it also encompasses decision-making by a designated Proxy, and substituted judgment on the part of both physician and proxy). Autonomy is thus a concept of respect for an individual, and the individual is its locus. This is a primarily a body of ethics concerned with the direct care of the patient.

BENEFICENCE: The concept of Beneficence is also centered on the individual and the behavior of the physician towards that person. But beneficence is an active principal: it involves *doing* good. However, Beneficence as an active principle does not merely yield control to another individual – the patient, or the patient's representative. Beneficence steps beyond the individual, and encompasses a broader, even a societal, field. Beneficence also takes into account the repercussions of an action for the patient's surround. For example, if one acts to prolong the life of a patient, but thereby impoverishes not only the patient but by extension the family of the patient, or if the decision leaves, say, an immediate caretaker – often a family member, or spouse - with an overwhelming burden of fulfilling needs and demands while simultaneously depriving that person of job opportunities and economic resources, is that beneficence? What constitutes true beneficence in a given case is a not infrequent topic of discussion in ethics committees.

NON-MALEFICENCE: The concept of Non-maleficence initially would seem to be redundant to the principal of Beneficence, but it is not. While it underpins it – since Hippocrates, a cornerstone of ethical behavior has been *primum non nocere*, or first do no harm - the principal of non-maleficence is essentially passive. But the mere absence of actively harming someone is not equivalent to beneficence: the absence of evil does not automatically insure the presence of good, or of doing good. Beneficence is active, not merely inactive or passive. Non-maleficence may be passive – an act of restraint, or non-action - but it also may be a body of ethics concerned with the repercussions of practice beyond the individual, or relating to the individual through societal mandates.

Violation of the principals of autonomy, non-maleficence and the requirement for beneficence overlapped notably in the infamous "bad 'blood" project initiated by the U.S. Public Health Service in 1932. At that time 600 poor black men were recruited into a project to study the natural history of syphilis. Although, in the 1940s, penicillin had been found to be an effective treatment, the affected men (there was a control group) were never offered or given this treatment, which did them harm - a violation of both non—malevolence and beneficence. Further, the untreated men infected others, and children with congenital syphilis were conceived and born. (The project continued to be funded until 1972, when a whistle-blower caused such unfavorable publicity that it was ended).

The positions of physicians and societies of physicians concerning policy formation and the administration of health care involve autonomy and both beneficence and non-maleficence. For instance, the American Medical Association considers it unethical for a physician to assist in executions. That is still a one-on-one interaction, but it would take place by legal, and hence societal, mandate. Beyond the act itself, which certainly removes autonomy, or choice – most persons would surely prefer not to be executed - it is not beneficial to that individual as we generally understand the meaning of the word beneficial and it does do harm to that person. It also has implications for societal and legal attitudes – it validates the practice of execution. Another example of course would be legislation banning abortion, which not only removes autonomy (the choice of an individual woman to have an abortion) but rebounds on a far larger group of persons; physicians, who would be in legal jeopardy for assisting the woman; family members, care-takers, other societal programs for various supports (which may or may not be there).

JUSTICE: the courtroom is a crucible where ethical responsibility to individuals and society meet. Above all, the courtroom is the place where truth must be told and acted upon. There is a body of literature about this also, but it is largely directed at the behavior of testifying physicians (in the medical literature) or about what constitutes evidence (in the legal literature). Originally, it principally concerned testimony in malpractice cases. It is difficult to get physicians to proceed as though they remembered that their primary responsibility is to the Judge, or the State, or the truth of the matter about another physician's practices or competence. Serving Justice, in a larger sense, is the most neglected aspect of medical ethics. There are several reasons for this but beyond self-interest – economic, reputational – it is because Physicianhood is a cult and a culture. Any anthropologist would recognize the training of physicians to be a prolonged adolescent initiation rite characterized by an Authoritarian chain of command, physical stress (long hours of work and sleep deprivation), enforced codes of dress and demeanor, the communality of shared food (the hospital cafeteria, where else are you going to go if you're on call), with imperatives and prohibitions of conduct (no drinking or drugging while in service). There are codewords and passwords: medical jargon is understood largely by the Initiates. Ever wonder what your doctor was talking about? If you are a doctor, how often have you had to pause in a larger conversational group, to explain what was just said? It's an instance of shared information limited to a certain group: We know, You don't. There are trials and tests before the acceptance into the Brotherhood (Brother-and-Sister-hood) with degrees and license granting. These shared miserable experiences in themselves enforce bonding and a code of loyalty to the cohort, and encourage a united front when any member is challenged. It is very hard to get a doctor to testify against another doctor, or to interject themselves on other than a group level into issues of practice. Unless the pay is sufficient. From time to time there will be a movement to enforce a code of ethics in malpractice cases by articulating, say, that testifying physicians should not accept cases on a contingency basis (i.e. the financial outcome of the case, to which their testimony will have contributed). Or, by seeking to establish panels of qualified experts in designated areas, rotating testifying members, and limiting reimbursement for such activity. These attempts do not come to fruition, and it remains true that enforcement is essentially non-existent. There are no penalties for violation, except perhaps reputationally.

A relatively more recent development in the arena of courtroom testimony is the physician in the role of expert witness, aside from malpractice cases. In the Freddie Gray case, Dr. Morris Mark Soriano, a neurosurgeon, testified for the prosecution, and Dr. Matthew Ammerman, neurosurgeon, for the defense. Both sides concerned themselves with the question of when Gray's spine was broken and hence who, at that time, was responsible.

Guidelines for behavior are not the same thing as standards for competency. The American College of Legal Medicine (ACLM) has published clear Guidelines for the Expert Witness. As far back as the mid-19th century the American Medical Association (AMA) articulated a code of ethics which included, among other things, the obligation of a testifying physician to be informed about the subject matter. In other words, you are supposed to know what the hell you are talking about. This is vital in issues which do not rest upon experimental evidence or formal studies, but upon experience and the authority that derives therefrom. It is also important to be up on the pertinent literature. In this regard the expert witness for the prosecution, Matthew Ammerman, appeared to be woefully inadequate. Ammerman's testimony was based on clinical opinion - his own. It did not derive from formal studies or reported series of cases.

It was not informed by basic physiology or the experience of other experts when he was outside his field of knowledge, such as the ability to speak despite diaphragmatic paralysis, which is well recognized, or the subject of seizures caused by oxygen deprivation, which is also standard knowledge. Forensic Pathologist Allan affirmed both of these points in her testimony as a witness, and both could have been easily verified by consultation with Ammerman's pulmonary and neurological colleagues. He could have walked down the hall and asked somebody. Most of all, it Ammerman's testimony was flawed by a simple failure of logic in observation that would have been within the grasp of a grade-schooler. He was inferring function at an earlier state of injury from changes after manipulations, procedures, and the natural progression of injury more than a week after the event. He spoke as though what was seen at autopsy represented the initial injury, not the well-recognized secondary stages of tissue change. He misquoted autopsy findings. Had he reviewed Gray's hospitalization records, as he said he did, he might have noted that Gray had been given anticonvulsants for repetitive seizures after he was admitted – though Ammerman in sworn testimony said that it would have been impossible for Gray to have seized after injury in the van, as brains deprived of oxygen could not seize. But he had an academic appointment, and the Brotherhood of physicians would not speak out against him or talk to investigative reporters. Despite the conversations that went on among spine surgeons at Hopkins, the University of Maryland and elsewhere, neither individuals nor Neurosurgical Departments spoke out audibly about either the announcement of the charges or the errors of Ammerman's testimony.

Ammerman's testimony was shockingly at variance with what is known about spinal cord injury and its consequences. He had a decent reputation as a spine surgeon, and a nice courtroom manner. And at his back, the Brotherhood of spine surgeons at the medical schools, holding meetings about what had really happened, but ever reluctant to criticize one of their own. The prosecutors of course did not challenge him: he was their guy, helping to place the timing of injury to the van ride and hence to fix the responsibility on those charged. Attorneys Schazow and Bledsoe may well have known better, from the evidence of the arrest video – how could they not see what was before their eyes, how could they not listen to the accounts of the eye- witnesses? But they were stuck with the charges they had to bring. The Defense didn't speak out: although he was placing responsibility on their clients, Ammerman was also helping to lead the prosecution down a path of circumstantial evidence which they doubtless knew would not stand up. Mosby was correct in saying that they could try the same case 100 times, without a different outcome.

All of this is to say that there is another, very largely unaddressed, area of ethical responsibility for individual physicians. That is the moral obligation to speak out, and to offer voluntary input, professional but unreimbursed, in individual and obvious cases. To step away from Freddie Gray for a moment, let us think about another illustrative example from Baltimore:

In 2012, a black man named Anthony Anderson was coming out of a food store with a bag in each hand. A video exists in which two independent eye-witnesses recounted the same story in detail. Without preamble, two officers jumped him from behind, knocked him down, began to kick him, and kicked him to death. He was taken to hospital where he was found to have multiple blunt force injuries: to his head, to his torso with 8 fractured ribs, and a lacerated spleen, from which he bled out into his abdomen and died. The case was ruled a homicide, but the officers were not charged. They were briefly suspended, with pay. The police said he died because he choked on drugs. This was not mentioned in the autopsy report, although distinctive findings would have identified death from choking. Police investigation found that no excessive force had been used. The family sued, and were paid $300,000.

Given the witness documentary video which can still be seen on Youtube, and given the autopsy findings, it would have been absolutely clear to anyone with any basic let alone medical knowledge that he had died as a result of an unprovoked police assault. Even were it provoked – the police claimed he was doing a drug deal – there was absolutely no reason to brutalize him. He did not resist arrest. He died because they kicked him so hard and repeatedly that they broke 8 of his ribs and lacerated his spleen and he bled out into his abdomen – that was an autopsy finding – and he died from that. But where were the voices from physicians, collectively or as individuals?

Some did speak out on Freddie Gray: we do not know how many and are not going to be allowed to find out. A letter generated to the listserve of the American Academy of Neurology, urging commentary concerning the timing of Gray's injury, resulted in an unknown number of responses to Mosby giving the opinions of physicians that his neck was broken by the arresting officers and before the van ride. Some individuals with excellent credentials contacted Mosby's office. It was, however, too late for the charges to be reversed. What is certain nonetheless is that Mosby had multiple communications from physicians stating that in their professional opinions, Gray's neck had been broken during the arrest. Those whose raised their voices deserve commendation. Those who did not were, and are, guilty of breaches of the ethics of their profession, and of their responsibility to society and to justice.

In November 2015, the venerable New England Journal of Medicine (NEJM) published an editorial entitled *Graduate Medical Education in the Freddie Gray Era*. The Authors were from the Johns Hopkins Bayview Center – serving East Baltimore – and spoke of the necessity for training Residents in the sociological determinants of healthcare. Since 2011 there had been a program there called *Medicine for the Greater Good*, which emphasized the social determinants of health. To quote the authors: "Since the conditions leading to health disparities are not unique to Baltimore, we believe that residency programs throughout the United States have a duty to raise awareness of the socioeconomic determinants of health and to train young physicians to recognize and change the circumstances responsible for poor health outcomes…in many ways, an emphasis on social justice and advocacy for the disadvantaged harkens back to a role historically embraced by physicians." Workshop topics for residents are listed, but social justice is a proposed, not a currently listed, topic. And nowhere mentioned is the subject of responsibility in facilitating social justice by individually coming forward when social justice is miscarried. But when that miscarriage is specifically related to incorrect medical assumptions and information, and that is known to the observers in the field, then it is a violation of medical ethics not to come forward. A letter to the Editor of the NEJM on the subject was declined. A letter to the Director of the program, inquiring about its outcomes, went unanswered.

As for the issue of informed Expert Witness testimony: individual specialty societies should establish panels of qualified witnesses as a pool with rotating membership. Testifying Experts should be required to disqualify themselves if a conflict of interest or other sources of bias can be identified, and they should be paid at a uniform and non-contingent rate.

———

If, in the end, the crucible of justice in the courts failed Freddie, there was plenty of blame to go around. The failure of the informed Neurosurgical community to come forward individually and collectively deserves blame. Mosby largely blamed the lack of independent investigation, the absence of Community oversight into the inquiry, the Police, and the Judge, saying that she could have tried the case a hundred times with no different outcome. She was entirely right with regard to the problem of Police investigating Police and their subordination of the Prosecution investigations. Losing witness testimony, among other things, is not pretty. But it is impossible not to assign her, along with Carol Allan and David Fowler, a large part of the responsibility for the outcome. Mosby herself, in tracking the misleading assessment of the Autopsy report without close reading of its separation of opinion from medical evidence, was ultimately to blame. Her charges were inappropriately conceived. She did not seek appropriate medical input before bringing them. She failed to insist on an independent investigation. And while Judge Williams could certainly be criticized for some of his decisions – most notably, on the seatbelting issue, but also in terms of his framing of the timing of Goodson's awareness of Gray's condition, he was honorable, experienced and competent. In ignoring the obvious video evidence and the testimony of eye-witnesses and by failing to charge the arresting officers specifically with homicide, Mosby must bear the major responsibility.

It didn't happen in the van. The arresting officers broke his neck.

The case should be retried.

AUTHOR

Mary Anne Whelan, Ph.D., MD, is a retired academic and clinical neurologist with a number of specialty-related publications and prior appointments at Bassett Medical Center, Columbia College of Physicians and Surgeons, and Dartmouth Medical School. She is currently a Fellow of the American Academy of Pediatrics, a member of the American Neurological Association, a member of the Child Neurology Society, an Editorial Board member of the Journal of Child Neurology, an *ad hoc* for other related medical journals, and a member of her hospital Ethics Committee. She was initially assisted in research by Maria Trovato, a student at the University of Maryland who is pursuing a double major in Multi-platform journalism and Government and Politics. Baltimore journalist Ericka Blount Danois contributed observations, commentary and guidance throughout. She may write her own book.